MONEY GAME$

THE BUSINESS OF SPORTS

ANN E. WEISS

Houghton Mifflin Company
Boston 1993

For Malcolm with love

Library of Congress Cataloging-in-Publication Data

Weiss, Ann E., 1943–
    Money games : the business of sports / Ann E. Weiss.
        p.   cm.
    Includes bibliographical references.
    Summary: Discusses the influence and growing importance of money
in the complex world of professional and amateur sports.
    ISBN 0-395-57444-7
    1. Sports—Economic aspects—United States.   2. Sports—United
States—Moral and ethical aspects.   3. Professional sports—Economic
aspects—United States.   4. Professional sports—United States—
Moral and ethical aspects.   5. Athletes—Professional ethics—
United States.   [1. Sports—Economic aspects.]   I. Title.
GV716.W45   1993   92-25002
338.47796—dc20   CIP
                           AC
Printed in the United States of America

AGM   10   9   8   7   6   5   4   3   2   1

Contents

Author's Note

When I started this book, Jose Canseco had just signed baseball's richest-ever contract. Twenty-three and a half million dollars over five years—it seemed like the ultimate sports salary. Then came Roger Clemens . . . Bobby Bonilla . . . Patrick Ewing . . . I found myself doing almost as much rewriting as writing.

Writing, then rewriting, and rewriting again, was to be the pattern for this book. In the time it took me to complete it, boxer Mike Tyson went from lionized former world heavyweight champion to convicted rapist. When I started chapter one, broadcast executives at CBS-TV were delighting in their new $1.06 billion deal to air major league baseball games between 1990 and 1994. Well before I launched into chapter eight, CBS's extravagant spending had helped to create record losses for the network. The cost of advertising time during a sports classic like the Super Bowl rose steadily as I worked, hitting $28,000 a *second* in 1992. Scandals rocked one college sports program after another. Two new National League baseball franchises were announced. American track star Mike Powell smashed the 23-year-old long jump record with a 29 foot 4 1/2 inch leap, a gain of two full inches. A single baseball trading card sold at auction for an astonishing $410,000. The nation of South Africa moved far enough away from its policy of strict racial separation to win an invitation to the International Olympic Games, its first in over two decades. From the pinnacle of athletic fame and fortune, Earvin "Magic" Johnson told the world that he had the virus that causes AIDS.

Rewriting continued as the book went into production. The modern "all-amateur" Olympics, grown increasingly professional over recent years, reached new levels of commercialism in 1992. The National Football League lost an important free agency case in court and, sensing money problems as a result, backed away from its planned 1994 expansion. Baseball team owners forced the resignation of Commissioner Fay Vincent. How many changes and how fast they had come.

By the time you read this, there will have been many more. Some, such as the changes that were sure to follow Vincent's departure, will take place behind the scenes. Others, like the loss of a superstar, will affect fans directly. As always in professional sports, many of the changes will be financial. There will be higher salaries, new television deals, more complex sponsorship arrangements. Sport is, after all, a business, and the bottom line for any business must be reckoned in dollars and cents.

But sport is more than just a business, and money is not its only object. So it is that sport's most important changes—the ones we will remember best and longest—will be those that take place on the field: the record-breaking performances, the unexpected victories and last-minute defeats, the athletic triumphs and tragedies, the sudden emergence of a bright young star. And so it should be, for in sport, the real bottom line is human striving, human competition, and human achievement.

—A.E.W.

Chapter 1

Soaring Salaries

Was the 1991 World Series baseball's best ever? Probably.

For starters, there were its unlikely contenders. The Minnesota Twins and the Atlanta Braves, each of which had finished 1990 at the bottom of its division, rose Cinderella-like through the standings to wind up in first place. During the league championship play-off series, Minnesota needed only five games to claim the American League crown. Over in the National League, Atlanta went the full seven games before winning the pennant.

But it was the Series itself that was the real thriller. Four of its seven games were decided on the final pitch—the first time that had happened in the Series' eighty-eight-year history. There were other records set as well. The '91 Series was the first with five games decided in the winning team's last turn at bat, the first in which three games went into extra innings, and the first to have its seventh game—the one that must produce the Series winner—remain a 0-0 tie through nine taut innings of play.

The tension was almost unbearable as the two teams came into the tenth inning of that final game. Atlanta pitcher John Smoltz had done an outstanding job through seven-and-a-third innings, giving up no runs and six hits, striking out four batters, and walking only one before being relieved from the bull pen. But the Twins' Jack Morris was sensational. Making his third start in nine days, the thirty-six-year-old shrugged off his manager's late-inning suggestions that he might be tiring. Already, he had posted nine complete innings of scoreless ball. Now he made it ten and headed back to the dugout.

Up to bat for the Twins in the bottom of the tenth came left fielder Dan Gladden. He doubled and went to third on a sacrifice. The next two men up received intentional walks. Then, as the hometown crowd roared, and Atlanta fans watched in anguish, pinch hitter Gene Larkin sent a fly ball over the Braves' infield and Gladden crossed home plate with the winning run. "Fitting Ending for a Storybook Series" was baseball writer Claire Smith's headlined conclusion in the *New York Times*. "Better Than This There Never Was," the *Times*'s sports columnist Ira Berkow agreed.

As far as Berkow was concerned, the '91 games weren't just the most thrilling World Series ever. They were unique in sports history, perhaps "the best sustained sporting event anyone has ever seen." He wasn't getting much of an argument from his fellow writers on that one. "The Series will forever be remembered," Claire Smith predicted. Murray Chass, also of the *Times,* added his voice to the chorus. A "scintillating" Series, he wrote, that built to a "crescendo of intensity" in a "succession of breathtaking games."

Nor were the games all that would take your breath away, Chass went on to inform his readers. Some upcoming money deals promised to leave fans equally winded. With the Series over, Morris's contract with the Twins was up for negotiation. Questions filled the sports pages. Would the veteran pitcher stay on with the Twins for the $3.65 million his old contract would have given him in 1992? Would he hold out for a higher salary with the Twins? Sign on with a more free-spending American League club? Accept a National League offer? How much might some other team think it worth to entice him away from Minneapolis?

The speculation had little to do with baseball itself, nor did it reflect what most Americans think of as the time-honored traditions of their national pastime. But it did hint at what many regard as a disturbing new aspect of the sport—its growing commercialism. All the financial talk, fans thought, suited a game in which being the best-paid has come to seem as important as being the best on the field, a game whose players compete as vigorously for dollars and cents as they do for hits and runs, a game increasingly focused upon money. Of course it's nothing new for players to want to be paid for their work. But until the 1990s, baseball salaries were modest—by today's standards. Two million dollars a year was about the most that even the best player could expect. Then, in November 1989, outfielder Rickey Henderson signed a $12 million four-year deal with the Oakland Athletics. At $3 million a year, Henderson ranked as the game's richest player.

For three days. That's how long it took for other team owners to hop on the contract bandwagon and set salaries skyrocketing. The New York Yankees offered slugger Don Mattingly $19 million over five years. Will Clark of the San Francisco Giants got $15 million over four years, and Henderson's teammate Dave Stewart won a two-year $7 million deal with the A's. Then, on June 27, 1990, Oakland's Jose Canseco put his name to the fattest contract in baseball history, one that promised to pay him $23.5 million over the next five years.

Twenty-three and a half million dollars! Three and a half million of that went to Canseco in the form of an immediate bonus. By 1995, the last year of the new contract, Canseco's salary alone was scheduled to hit $5.1 million. Special incentives could push the contract's final value past the $23.5 million figure. (Because of the varying ways incentives and bonuses are figured and paid out, it can be hard to say exactly how much a player is getting in any given year. That explains why news reports sometimes vary.)

The Canseco deal shattered every record anyone could think of. The big right fielder's signing bonus, added to his already-agreed-upon $2 million 1990 salary, turned him overnight into baseball's first $5 million-a-year player. His salary package sparked a round of heckling, much of it good-natured, among baseball's top earners. "That jerk," Will Clark called Canseco after the June signing. "I'm making a million more than you are," Canseco shot back, "you big, overrated, three-toed sloth with no arms." It was easy for Canseco to joke, but Rickey Henderson sounded a more serious note as he reacted to his teammate's good fortune. "I'm worth more than I get paid," the $12 million man groused. "I'm the only guy going to the Hall of Fame"—Henderson was assuming that he would be counted among baseball's immortals—"who makes that much less than Jose." It wasn't long before Henderson had new reason to feel jealous. Within six months, outfielder Darryl Strawberry had left the New York Mets to sign on with the Los Angeles Dodgers at $20.25 million over five years. Two months after that, the Boston Red Sox gave ace pitcher Roger Clemens a four-year contract worth $21.5 million. Late in 1991, the Mets signed Bobby Bonilla to a $29 million deal good through the 1996 season. Baseball has become a money game, no doubt about it.

So have other sports. Even before Canseco struck his landmark deal, football's Lawrence Taylor warned New York Giants team owners and managers that unless they were prepared to rewrite his contract, he wouldn't be showing up at training camp. Already the best-ever-paid linebacker in the National Football League (NFL) and slated to receive $1.21 million for the 1990–91 season, "L.T." was determined to become the first football defenseman to take home $2 million a year. He eventually settled for a $4.5 million contract good for three years. Highest paid in pro football by the end of the 1991–92 season was Miami Dolphins quarterback Dan Marino, at $5 million a year.

Basketball pros, too, are playing the money game. According to *Forbes* magazine, three U.S. basketball players ranked among the world's thirty richest athletes in 1990: Michael Jordan of the Chicago Bulls was earning $2.1 million a year. Earvin "Magic" Johnson of the Los Angeles Lakers—not yet aware that he was about to fall under the shadow of the disease AIDS (Acquired Immune Deficiency Syndrome)—was getting even more, $2.4 million a year, while the New York Knicks' Patrick Ewing was averaging $3.6 million a year over the life of his contract. The next year, the Knicks extended Ewing's contract with a six-year provision good for $33 million. Under the new deal, Ewing stood to earn $9.4 million in 1996 alone. Until Bobby Bonilla inked his deal with the Mets, Ewing was the highest-paid player in U.S. professional team sports.

Even in the National Hockey League (NHL), long the stingiest of professional team sports organizations, the first millionaires have hit the ice. Highest-paid in 1992, at $3.13 million a year over ten years, was Wayne Gretzky of the Los Angeles Kings. But others were doing all right, too. In June 1990, the St. Louis Blues signed high-scoring Brett Hull to a four-year, $7.1 million contract, then turned right around and offered defenseman Scott Stevens $5.1 million plus incentives over four years. The team's second multimillion-dollar offer—to a player considered good, but by no means a superstar—stunned the hockey world. "Flabbergasted" was how one sports agent described himself. This from someone whose very job it is to win deals just like Stevens's for his own athlete-clients. The president of the NHL's Vancouver Canucks—a man in the position of having to pay out on such contracts—used a different word: "Frightening."

Frightening? It's certainly true that athletes' incomes are escalating at a rate many consider out of control, and not just in team sports. Back in 1985, the first time Curtis Strange ranked as pro golf's top money-maker of the year, he earned half a million dollars. Three years later, Strange again led the Professional Golfers Association (PGA) in winnings—with $1.1 million. The record was promptly shattered by Tom Kite, who won $1.4 million in 1989. The year after that, Kite became the first PGA player to have earned more than $6 million over the course of his career. In 1992, record-high purses were being offered in the men's PGA Tour, the Senior PGA Tour for players over the age of fifty, and the Ladies PGA Tour.

The 1990s have been good to tennis, too. Ivan Lendl saw his lifetime earnings reach a record $16,282,293 as the decade began, and Monica Seles, the youngest-ever winner of the French Open tennis championship, walked away from that classic with $293,000 in 1990. That was just the beginning for Seles; the next year, she made over $2.6 million on the court. Legendary jockey Willie Shoemaker retired in 1990 to enjoy the $10 million he had banked in over four decades of horse racing, and U.S. bicyclist Greg LeMond won $360,000 for being first to finish the grueling 2,122-mile Tour de France. The nineties saw pro boxing champions getting $20 million just to climb into the ring to defend their titles. Challengers were paid less—$10 to $12 million per bout. Leading World Grand Prix auto racers were earning $8 or $9 million a year in prizes, while in stock car auto racing, a record five drivers won $1 million or more in 1990. "The cash register is ringing," as one official of the National Association of Stock Car Auto Racing (NASCAR) put it.

Nor is it ringing only at the track or on the court or inside the stadium. Sports stars lucky enough to win contracts to endorse commercial products can make it big in advertising as well. To the $2.1 million Michael Jordan earned handling basketballs in 1990, add the $6 million he got for advertising products ranging from Coca-Cola to Nike sneakers. In 1991, Jordan's off-court income jumped to $11 million—and that was *before* he signed an $18 million, ten-year deal to tout Gatorade, the "sports drink." Thirteen-year-old tennis whiz Jennifer Capriati of Florida became the game's youngest professional in 1990. She just as quickly became its youngest multimillionaire with a $1 million contract to advertise Prince tennis rackets and another $5 million in clothing endorsements. Monica Seles picked up an extra $800,000 in 1991 as the first sports star ever chosen to endorse a line of beauty products. No wonder *Sports Illustrated* magazine calls these the "days of the filthy-rich athlete."

Still—a team owner "frightened" at the thought of an athlete's multimillion-dollar contract? Nonsense, the athletes retort. As they see it, they aren't the only ones playing at money games. For owners, promoters, and organizers, too, they say, the cash registers sound their merry tune.

Take stock car racing. NASCAR track owners may be handing out generous purses, but they are also raking it in at the gate. More than three million fans could be counted upon to fill the stands at twenty-nine NASCAR races as the 1990s began, a per-event attendance greater than that averaged by pro football and major-league baseball put together. And these fans were paying $30, $40—up to $63—apiece for their seats. Or consider horse racing. Willie Shoemaker took home

$10 million over his long career. But his mounts brought in over twelve times that for their owners and backers.

Indications are that men and women on the ownership and management side of things are doing well in other sports. A single courtside seat for a Portland Trail Blazers basketball game cost $150 in 1990–91, double what it had been the year before. Multiply $150 times the number of seats sold at that price over the course of a season and the result is a good chunk of cash for the team's owners. Of course, the Trail Blazers club itself represents a considerable asset and so do other professional sports organizations. When baseball's National League announced plans to expand from twelve to fourteen teams in 1993, it set the price of each new franchise at a minimum of $95 million. An established club like the Los Angeles Dodgers has an estimated value of $225 million, says *Sports Illustrated.* It's a money game at the front office, too.

It's a money game all along the line. A heavyweight boxer may pick up $10 or $20 million for a fight, but only after his promoter signs a television contract worth $30 million or more. The United States Tennis Association (USTA) was rumored to have set a $50 million price tag on television broadcasting rights to its 1991 Open championship. But that sum was peanuts compared to what television, network, and cable combined agreed to pay the NFL in return for the privilege of airing its 1990–93 seasons—$3.6 *billion.* A single network, CBS, sunk $1.06 billion into purchasing the rights to major-league baseball games between 1990 and 1994.

Where does television find that sort of cash? In advertising. For each second of commercial airtime during a sportscast as widely watched as an NFL Super Bowl game, a network can ask for—and get—over $28,000. That works out to $1.7 million a minute. In 1992, broadcasters were squeezing twenty-eight minutes of commercials into every NFL game, up from about twenty-five minutes at the end of the 1980s.

Twenty-eight times $1.7 million . . . and all in the course of a few hours on a Sunday afternoon. That's money, real money. It's the kind of money that pays athletes their enormous salaries and makes professional franchises so valuable. It's the kind of money that fuels modern sports. And sometimes distorts and corrupts it in the process.

Chapter 2

From Games to Sport

The striker steps into position and readies his bat. Staring down at the other team's pitcher forty-five feet away, he indicates the spot where he wants the ball to come in. The pitcher delivers an underhand toss and whoosh! The ball sails past the striker a good half foot from where he expected it to be. Scowling, the striker lowers his bat, but before he can protest, the umpire steps forward and orders the pitcher to throw the ball again—and this time, to keep it where the striker has signaled. That's the rule of the game. Anyway, it's the rule in this town.

In other towns, the rules are different. Some umpires do let pitchers try to get strikers out by fooling them about where the pitch will be. Some playing fields are arranged so that the pitcher stands closer to sixty feet away from the strikers or, as people are beginning to dub them, "batters." Playing fields vary in size as well, and so do teams. Some teams have nine players; some have more. People can't even agree on what to call the game. It used to be known as "rounders" after the old English base-running game from which it derives. Later, recalling that the new game developed in the cities of the Northeast, some began referring to it as town ball or the Massachusetts game. Now, most use a more up-to-date term: base-ball.

The year is 1867.

If we can see differences between base-ball 125 years ago and baseball today, we can also spot similarities. Then as now, the game was popular around the country and among people in all walks of life. It was, and is, enjoyed by players and spectators alike. As far back as 1867, baseball news and scores filled newspaper columns. In fact, one baseball-only paper had just made its appearance. In 1866, the Hartford, Connecticut, *Bat and Ball* became the first publication to be devoted exclusively to what it was already hailing as America's "national game."

Baseball then and baseball now had something else in common: money. Up until 1867, most players were not paid formal salaries, although a few had their expenses quietly covered by team managers or backers. Other players might receive an occasional under-the-table gift. In a few cases, an outstanding prospect was lured to a particular town—and to a position on its team—by the offer of a job in that town. Typically, such a job would carry higher-than-average wages while still allowing its holder plenty of free time for play and practice. Then, in 1867, a Cincinnati team known as the Red Stockings proposed paying some of its members directly in return for their work on the field. Four Cincinnati players signed professional contracts that year. What had been merely a game was well on its way to becoming something else—a modern sport.

To distinguish between a sport and a game may seem strange, but sports historians tell us that a difference does exist. And while they admit that they—like the rest of us—tend to use the two words interchangeably, they add that sport in the modern sense has certain characteristics that set it apart from the games of earlier ages.

Our word "sport," says Richard D. Mandell, history professor at the University of South Carolina, did not even come into popular usage until a century or two ago. The word derives from the French *desporter,* commonly used to refer to the hunting of wild animals. Only gradually, between about 1750 and 1850, did the word assume its present meaning, which Mandell defines as "competitive activity of the whole human body according to sets of rules for purposes . . . set apart from the serious essential aspects of life."

Another historian, Allen Guttmann of Amherst College in Massachusetts, echoes Mandell's assertion that modern sport is separate from life's more useful pursuits. Sport consists, he says, of "nonutilitarian physical contests." It is meant to be enjoyed for itself and itself alone, rather than as a means of reaching some goal or other.

Guttmann further agrees with Mandell that our concept of "sport" is relatively new, adding that the word as we use it is rare even today in cultures so remote as to be cut off from twentieth-century ideas and customs. According to both Guttmann and Mandell, what we call sport was invented in England during the 1700s and 1800s, then greatly elaborated upon in the United States. Games go back to prehistoric times. And although long-ago games reflected instinctive forms of human behavior—and were no doubt fun—they were, quite often, played for definite and serious reasons.

Even among animals, play is productive as well as instinctive and entertaining. A kitten stalks a twig, pokes at it, bats it into the air, and pounces on it again and again. Obviously, she delights in what she is doing. Yet at the same time, her play is preparing her to be an efficient hunter. Puppies tussle with one another, yapping and biting. They seem to enjoy such behavior—they indulge in it often enough—but they are also learning how to protect themselves in a real fight.

The earliest human beings must have done much the same,

scuffling together like puppies and engaging in catlike running and chasing. Having the advantage of hands that could grasp and hold, they must also have developed throwing games. Primitive peoples would have enjoyed such activities as much as kittens and puppies do. But at the same time they, like young animals, learned from their play, gaining from it practice in the skills needed to survive in a difficult and dangerous world.

Ages passed and people, unlike animals, elaborated upon their games. Mandell cites horse racing, rope-swinging, stilt-walking, surfboarding, and snowshoe racing as examples of games that go back 12,000 years or more. Some sports historians believe these primitive games were consciously devised as ways of fine-tuning mankind's survival skills, though Mandell suggests they may simply have been meant for fun.

Other games, though, clearly had a purpose beyond recreation. Casual stick and rock throwing turned into target practice with deadly spearlike weapons. In prehistoric China and Japan, men fashioned bows and arrows and held archery contests as part of their military training. Rough-and-tumble scuffling was refined and hedged in by rules. Scenes sculpted ages ago in what are now Iran and Iraq depict warriors being instructed in boxing and wrestling. Racing and weight-lifting games were formalized around the world as ways of increasing endurance, speed, and agility.

Still other games had a more profound purpose. Take the Olympic Games of ancient Greece, for example. The first Olympiad is believed to have been staged in the Greek city-state of Elis in 776 B.C., and the games were replayed more or less regularly every four years for the next ten centuries. From all over Greece came the men of important families—no women allowed, even as spectators—to represent their cities in the various athletic events. ("Athletic" and "athlete" come from the Greek *athlos*—contest—and *athlon*—prize.) Yet the ancient Olympics were not primarily physical competitions aimed at weeding out losers or producing winners. They were religious festivals meant to honor the gods. Each set of games lasted five days, with boxing, wrestling, and racing contests interspersed with animal sacrifices and other religious rituals. At the games' conclusion came more ceremonial processions and banquets.

Prizes might be handed out at these final festivities. But since the point of the games was not so much to win a victory as it was to please the gods and gain their favor, the rewards were less for an athlete's physical accomplishments than for his spiritual ones. A successful wrestler might be honored for his graceful performance, or for the worthiness of his sacrifice or the eloquence of his prayer, but little attention would be paid to how often he had pinned his opponent to the ground. No one kept count of how many times a boxer scored a knockdown or noted when a runner set a new mark for speed. In fact, says Guttmann, the Greeks of 2,500 years ago had no word to describe someone who breaks a record. Nor did they bother to class athletes according to weight or size or to group distance runners as separate from sprinters. In games played for religious ends, physical inequalities were as irrelevant as physical supremacy.

As the centuries passed, though, games once played as a form of worship began to lose some of their religious significance. Olympic athletes began to regard winning as being as important as performing, and by the last few centuries B.C., some were going so far as to pay off their opponents or bribe the judges in order to secure victory. The trend toward the secular quickened its pace as the city-state of Rome gained power in the ancient world.

By the first century A.D., the Roman Empire stretched from

the area around the Black Sea in the east to England in the west, from Germany in the north into Africa to the south. Seizing an empire that size—and holding onto it through periodic uprisings—required a well-trained army, and Rome's emperors relied upon activities like boxing and wrestling to provide much of that training.

Rome's emperors had another purpose in encouraging what they, at any rate, thought of as games: maintaining the peace at home. Many Romans were fed up with perpetual warfare—and with paying the taxes needed to support it. To distract them from their grievances, the emperors sponsored the fantastic and horrifying contests known as circuses.

Judging by their enthusiasm for this form of entertainment, the Romans of 2,000 years ago were a bloodthirsty bunch. Circuses were set in large oval rings—*circus* means "ring" in Latin—surrounded by tiers of screaming, frenzied spectators. As the audience watched, boxers battled to the death. Armed men slaughtered one another. Savage beasts tore at each other's flesh, and sometimes, in contests deliberately designed to be unequal, at human flesh as well. Small armies of gladiators—swordsmen—fought, and fell, and were replaced by new armies. Performances might last for months, with as many as 10,000 men and a like number of animals perishing in each. Not until A.D. 681 were circuses abolished.

By that time, the Roman Empire had collapsed, the victim of repeated invasions by tribes from central and eastern Europe. The Middle Ages, the years from the fall of Rome to about 1400, were beginning.

Just as the mention of ancient Rome brings to mind that city's terrible circuses, so the phrase "Middle Ages" recalls the games called tournaments. Knights in shining armor and their lavishly outfitted ladies; plunging, snorting horses; the clash of lances; a violent melee; recovery of the dead and wounded—such were the elements of these medieval war games. Although tournaments were not sacred events in the manner of the ancient Olympics, they were celebrations of the ideals of Christian knighthood, conducted under rules that called for contestants to display such virtues as piety, loyalty, courage, and courtesy.

Galas as elaborate as this were for the great and powerful only. Medieval Europeans believed that God had created some people to be rich and others to be poor and that it was part of his design for the world that the two groups should never mix. This belief found its way into law, and peasants caught trying to ape their betters, even in their games, might be harshly punished. The lower classes had their own diversions. Running and jumping games were popular. So were those that entailed kicking or hitting a ball-like object. The ball might be made of wood or cork, or it might be an inflated animal bladder—even a skull accidentally unearthed from some ancient burying ground. Such rough pastimes had few rules, only local traditions, and even those traditions varied according to the number of players and their individual skills, the size and shape of the available playing space, and so on. No one played a particular position; whole villages of men, women, and children tumbled about together. They played at some risk, however, since royalty did its best to discourage such games. Of what use was a peasant's skill with a ball? Repeatedly, European kings issued edicts forbidding football and ordering archery contests in its place. Good bowmen were always in demand in time of war.

Football and jousting were not the only games officially off limits to the peasantry. Hunting—even when its purpose was not pleasure, but the gathering of food—was forbidden, often on pain of death. None but great landowners might disport themselves. Furthermore, even as the Middle Ages drew to a close, peasants found new games—ancestors of modern bowling, golf, and tennis—denied them as well. Under a 1388 English law, "court-tennis" might not be played by servants or laborers. The law was renewed in 1410 and again in the next century. Also in the 1500s, lawn bowling was prohibited to all but nobles and those "having manors, lands or tenements, to the yearly value of one hundred pounds or above." The prohibition was repeated in 1618.

By 1618, the first English settlers—high-born and low— had arrived in America. With them came their games. At first, the colonists hemmed those games in with the class-conscious laws of their native land. Hunting as an amusement was to remain a rich man's sport. So was horse racing. As late as 1674, a tailor in the Virginia colony was fined for having dared to enter his horse in a race against a gentleman's.

But rules meant to maintain class distinctions in games were harder to enforce in the New World than they had been in the Old. In England, racehorses were thoroughbreds, expensive to buy and costly to feed and maintain. Few tailors would have been able to afford one. In America, small, sturdy horses were readily available and pasturage cheap. Almost anyone could own a horse. And race it. Formal hunting parties might be just for the wealthy, but almost everyone hunted for food. The lines of separation blurred as working Americans moved in on the aristocratic pastimes formerly the preserve of the upper class.

They blurred further as the well-off adopted the amusements of farmers, laborers, and servants. Wealthy English boys might scorn games like football and rounders, but their social equals in the colonies, faced with a less-formal lifestyle and a shortage of polished companions, joined right in. By the time the colonies won their independence in 1783, American boys and men (but not girls and women, or blacks or Native Americans of either sex) were pretty much united in the games they played together.

They were also about to become united in the sports they enjoyed. For by the second half of the eighteenth century, sport—sport in the modern sense—was emerging. Its appearance was one aspect, sports historians say, of the scientific, technological, economic, and social upheaval we call the Industrial Revolution.

The Industrial Revolution, which lasted from about 1750 to around 1850, transformed Western civilization. The first changes came in science and technology. Steam engines took the place of less efficient water- or wind-driven machines. Factories run on steam could turn out large quantities of goods far more quickly and cheaply than most people had ever imagined possible. More and more factories sprang up, and as they did, thousands of men and women left their ancestral farms and villages and moved to the cities to look for manufacturing jobs. A new industrial working class had been created. So had a new class of capitalists—those with enough money, capital—to establish a business and keep it running.

At the factory, other changes awaited. Work there was not organized like work in the village. In his village shop, the cobbler had started with a hide of leather. He cut it, shaped it, and stitched it into a pair of shoes. The weaver started with an empty loom and finished with a bolt of cloth. But in the factory, no single worker saw a project through from beginning to end. All cooperated as a group, each specializing in a small isolated part of the production process. Some threaded the looms; others ran the machinery that drove the shuttle; still others cut away the finished bolt of cloth.

As specialists, workers could not be responsible for the overall quality of the finished goods. Responsibility for that belonged to factory owners—and to the overseers, assistants, and supervisors they hired to manage day-to-day operations. Management set the standards and made the rules. The shift from individual responsibility to bureaucratic management and rule-making was yet another change of the Industrial Revolution.

Still other changes were the ones taking place in people's beliefs about themselves and their world. Even after the Middle Ages, social and economic class distinctions remained clear-cut and widely respected. But in the urban workplace, people of all sorts were thrown together, leading to the exchanging of ideas and the sharing of customs. Old notions began to crumble, and as the 1800s began, the public attitude was increasingly democratic. It was also, due largely to the new interest in science, more secular than it had been in the devoutly religious Middle Ages.

The emphasis on science brought with it another change— a growing fascination with numbers. Numbers were the "language" of the science and technology that underlay the Industrial Revolution. Numbers soon became the language of the factory as well. Managers set production quotas and measured a worker's worth in terms of speed and quantity of output. Numbers also served as tools for comparing past performances with present and helped in setting goals for future achievements. However much a factory produced in one year, the aim was to produce more the next and more again after that. As industrialization continued and productivity did increase, people came to see material progress as a natural and inevitable part of life.

Faith in the idea of progress and a preoccupation with numbers. A new secularism and sense of democracy. Specialization, rules, and bureaucratic organization. Those were the characteristics of the new industrial age and, Guttmann says, of modern sport as well. Taken together, these seven characteristics define what we know as sport and distinguish it from the games of earlier ages.

Certainly, modern sport is secular, lacking even the semi-religious quality of the medieval tournament. It is democratic in that, theoretically at least, it permits participation regardless of wealth or social origin. Some "rich men's games" like polo or yachting may be financially out of reach of most people, but they are not legally off-limits to anyone. Modern sports, unlike the games of ancient times, also provide equal conditions of competition. Boxers are classed by weight; contenders in other events are grouped by age or ability. "Fair play" is a hallmark of modern sport.

So is specialization. Gone are the days when marathon racers also ran sprints or whole villages turned out to scramble after a ball. No one today expects a championship diver to win a swimming race or a football quarterback to shine on defense.

Specialization, on the field or in the factory, calls for teamwork and rules. Not the unchangeable, god-given rules of ritual games nor the loose traditions of medieval football, but the kind of detailed regulations that make modern tennis the same game in New York that it is in Los Angeles—or in London or Tokyo. The precise, specific rules of modern sports cover just about every imaginable aspect of play, leaving almost nothing up to the individual. But since these rules are written by people, they may be altered by them to suit the needs of players or the preferences of fans—even the demands of television and its advertisers.

Modern sports organizations are also unique to today's world. Of course, it took organization to put on an Olympiad or stage a tournament. But orchestrating the occasional spectacle is only a small part of what our sports bureaucracies do. Those bureaucracies—made up of trainers, coaches, managers, referees, umpires, medical personnel, club owners, league officials, association members, commissioners, and all the rest—oversee all aspects of a sport: directing practices, supervising play, approving equipment and facilities, arranging schedules and play-offs, writing and enforcing rules, disciplining, amassing and verifying records and statistics.

Records and statistics. If there is one thing above all that sets modern sport apart from the games of earlier ages, it is sport's passion for measuring physical accomplishment in terms of numbers. When the Olympic Games were revived in their modern form in 1896, all of its competitions were scored numerically. All, that is, but gymnastics. The gymnasts' dancelike routines did not lend themselves to judgment by numbers, a fact that led one American to ask whether theirs could be said to represent a "real" sport. The introduction of a ten-point scoring system quickly settled that question, and today's gymnasts are rated right down to the third decimal place. Numbers are central to every other modern sport as well.

Record keeping—or rather, record *breaking*—is equally central. As we know, the ancient Greeks gave no thought to records. The Romans had little use for them either, nor did the men and women of medieval Europe. According to Guttmann, the English noun "record," signifying "unsurpassed quantified achievement," was not commonly heard until the 1880s. Now, a century later, it's major news when a runner shaves as little as a thousandth of a second off the time for a race. When, in 1991, American Mike Powell demolished the twenty-three-year-old world long-jump record of 29 feet 2 1/2 inches with a 29 foot 4 1/2 inch leap, the *New York Times* heralded his triumph in inch-high type. But even such a headline fades fast as athletes and fans set their sights on the next record. That it will come eventually they have no doubt. Progress demands that every performance, even the most spectacular, be improved upon, and belief in progress is one of sport's most enduring legacies from the Industrial Revolution.

But much as the social and intellectual ideas of the Industrial Revolution did to shape sport, they were not the only forces prompting its development. Helping in a different way were the technological changes of the age.

One technological contribution came in 1839 when the American Charles Goodyear discovered a way to turn rubber, which in its natural state is difficult to shape and mold, into its tough, elastic "vulcanized" form. Vulcanization had implications for a number of sports, tennis among them. Originally a game in which players used the palm of the hand to bat a ball back and forth across a net, tennis (initially known as sphairistike, from the Greek "ball-playing") adopted rubberized balls, along with strung racquets and the first more or less modern courts, in 1874. New and improved materials helped modernize other games. In 1848, golfers gave up their lifeless "featheries," bags of leather stuffed with birds' feathers, for springy balls made with gutta-percha and, after 1898, rubber. Golf, which had developed out of a variety of games— some played within confines as narrow as an alleyway—became a sport of expansive, countrylike courses. Soft cloth baseballs gave way to hard cork-and-rubber cored stitched leather models, and footballs, too, were now made of leather. Some new inventions meant whole new sports. Patented ball bearings turned roller skating into a fad in the 1880s. Another product of that decade, the internal combustion engine, led to the earliest automobiles—and auto racing.

Other types of inventions played yet another role in promoting modern sport. Railroads allowed players and teams to move around freely, competing on a countrywide basis and recasting local spur-of-the-moment games as prearranged contests of national interest. Furthermore, since few people had sufficient athletic talent to justify traveling long distances at considerable cost in order to take part in such contests, modern sports developed as events that men and women were more likely to watch than to play.

Other inventions helped turn traditional village free-for-alls into spectator sports. The telegraph—and later, the telephone—brought sports home to anyone who wanted to follow the action, no matter how far away it happened to be taking place. By the 1880s, pool halls and bars across America were equipped to receive up-to-the-minute news about baseball, racing, and boxing. Cheap newspapers and magazines kept sports fans informed about events near and far, the papers' number-laden pages feeding the public appetite for records and statistics.

Not only did the new modes of transportation and communication permit sport to flourish, they also tended to reenforce those particular aspects of modern sport that made it so much a reflection of the modern industrialized world. Impossible for teams from cities hundreds of miles apart to compete unless they could agree on common sets of rules, standard playing fields and equipment, and a single vocabulary. Pointless to travel long distances at considerable expense unless each side was determined to win. Easier to win with teamwork and cooperation, each player specializing in the skill he was best at, yet each obeying the orders of a manager who had the overall team goal—victory—foremost in mind. Foolish to field a team that did not include the most talented players available, whatever their economic or social background. (Although some early organizers did just that foolish thing and the racial integration of sports was still decades away—and is by no means complete today.) Unthinkable to celebrate one single religion in a spectacle aimed at entertaining the mixed populace of a modern industrialized nation.

As the 1880s began, most of the sports we know today

were in place. Practically without exception, they were English in origin. "Almost all the field events of a track meet were invented by English university students," Mandell says. "They invented the running broad jump, the triple jump, the hurdles, and steeplechase races. They also established the standard track distances. Englishmen set the distances for swimmers, for rowing competitions, and for horse races of all kinds . . . They . . . 'invented' [wrote the rules for] almost all the team games now played . . . built the first sporting yachts, racing sculls, and row boats for trained crews. They also devised the first football goal posts, boxing gloves, stopwatches, and most other sporting equipment." They refined medieval-style football into its most popular European forms, soccer and rugby. And they did all this over a remarkably brief period of time. "It is easy to forget," Mandell wrote in a book published in 1984, "that most of the events, games, and equipment of modern sport are not much more than a hundred years old."

From England, sport traveled to the United States. Rounders made the journey early. So did crew, and in 1852 a race between one group of rowers from Harvard and another from Yale became the first intercollegiate sporting event held in America. U.S. students began playing soccer and rugby in the 1860s, with the first college game taking place in 1869. The distinctly American style of football emerged on college campuses around 1880—to the initial horror of university officials who found its violence appalling.

Other sports took on a New World flavor. In the 1850s, English soldiers stationed in Canada adapted field hockey to a northern climate, and within twenty years, ice hockey was a college sport in that country. There and in the northern United States, hockey had a great advantage: it could be played when the weather was too cold for most other games.

So eager, in fact, were fans for sports they could enjoy year round that in 1891 James Naismith, a physical education teacher in Massachusetts, sat down to invent a winter game as active and exciting as a summer one, yet playable indoors. Having at his disposal a gymnasium with a balcony, two peach baskets, and a soccer ball, Naismith attached the baskets to balcony railings at either end of the gym, drafted thirteen rules of play, and tossed the ball onto the court. Basketball had been born.

Like football, basketball succeeded as a college sport first and only later as a professional one. By 1905, there were basketball teams at more than forty U.S. colleges and universities. The first pro teams had appeared in 1895, but those teams repeatedly fell apart to be replaced by others. Still, just seven years after basketball's invention, six professional teams were competing against each other on a semiregular basis. What enabled the new sport to organize so quickly? The answer, oddly enough, lies in baseball and what happened to it in the 1860s and 1870s.

We've already had a glimpse of baseball in the late 1860s: a game of mostly unsalaried amateurs who ran their own clubs, followed local rules, did their own scheduling, and took to the field under somewhat chaotic conditions. Not that players hadn't made some attempt to systematize. In 1858, members of twenty-two clubs had joined together to form the National Association of Base Ball Players. But although the National Association survived for over ten years, it never did manage to write or enforce consistent rules.

Yet baseball continued to gain popularity. A growing number of fans even proved willing to pay good money to watch games, making it possible for players to buy the more sophisticated equipment coming onto the market. Another source of funds was the business community. Sports-minded merchants or others might offer to sponsor a team, providing uniforms or enabling managers to offer discreet subsidies to their best players. In 1869, the Cincinnati Red Stockings became baseball's first fully paid professional squad.

The Red Stockings traveled 11,877 miles in 1869, playing sixty-nine games—without losing one—in front of 200,000 spectators. Gate receipts amounted to $29,726.26. However, since player salaries came to $9,500 while other expenses swallowed up $20,224.87 more, the season was less than a financial triumph for the club. It folded the next year.

The team's former manager, Harry Wright, resurfaced in Boston in 1871. Wright now turned his talents—and the strong pitching arm of a young man named Albert Spalding—to making the *Boston* Red Stockings the nation's top team. At the same time, Wright and others set up a professional players' group to take over for the failed amateur association. The new National Association of Professional Base Ball Players represented a revived effort to regularize the game and turn it into a serious money-maker. But to its organizers' disappointment, the second National Association accomplished little beyond adopting standard-sized baseballs.

More noteworthy were Association failures, which included its inability to produce top-quality play. The group did sponsor an annual championship series, games intended to arouse public enthusiasm and send ticket sales soaring. But since Association rules allowed any team that could come up with a $10 entry fee to participate in its play-offs, a powerful club like Boston—seventy-one wins against eight losses in 1875— could find itself facing such a hopeless cause as the Brooklyn Atlantics, 2-42 over the same season. Not a lot of thrills in such an unequal contest. Not many ticket buyers, either.

Just as disappointing was the Association's inability to stop member teams from raiding one another's player rosters.

During the 1875 season, for example, a Chicago club signed a number of Boston players, including team captain Albert Spalding, to 1876 contracts. Making such advance deals went against the rules, but that fact didn't bother Spalding and his new friends in the Windy City. They were working on a plan to put the Association behind them—and to put baseball, once and for all, on a solid financial footing.

Their plan called for replacing the players' organization with a National League of Professional Baseball Clubs. Or, as sports reporter Leonard Koppett would have it, the National *League* of Professional Baseball *Clubs.* "It was the last word that changed everything," Koppett wrote in his book, *Sports Illusion, Sports Reality.* The move took baseball out of the hands of its players and gave it to the clubs—in the person of their sponsors and backers. This transfer was deliberate, a recognition, Spalding later explained, of the distinction between capital and labor. From now on, backers—owners—would supply the money while players did the work. Together the two would offer the public the genuinely competitive product it craved. Baseball would be in business.

And in a monopoly business at that. Monopolies—the word comes from the Greek *monos,* "alone," and *polein,* "to sell"—were common in the world of nineteenth-century American business. Also known as trusts or cartels, monopolies are arrangements under which a group gets exclusive ownership of a commodity or a service (sugar or oil or telephone lines—or baseball) and controls it absolutely. The costs of production, the amount to be offered for sale, the price to consumers, all are decided upon ahead of time by members of the cartel.

From the outset, the National League (NL) owners were determined to make theirs the only game in town. They, and they alone, would hire players, write rules, draw up schedules, set ticket prices (at 50¢ each), pay umpires ($5 per game), arrange play-offs (complete with a banner, or pennant, "costing not less than $100" for the winning club), and maintain records. And they would keep baseball—and its profits—strictly to themselves.

How to accomplish all that? First, by limiting the number of clubs in the league. Originally there were eight: Chicago, St. Louis, Hartford, Boston, Louisville, New York, Philadelphia, and Cincinnati. Membership fluctuated over the years, but even its 1993 expansion leaves the NL with just fourteen teams. The owners also took care to establish a territorial monopoly for each club. One city—one team—that was to be the rule (though between 1900 and 1958, New York City was allowed its Giants, who played in the borough of Manhattan, and its Dodgers, happily ensconced in Brooklyn). Territorial monopolies meant teams no longer had to compete among themselves for local fan support. Anyone who wanted to see big-league play had no choice but to buy an NL team ticket.

Making sure NL play really was big-league, seriously competitive, and therefore truly exciting was the number-one challenge facing club owners. Meeting it required finding a way to keep the teams balanced at more or less equal strength. To achieve equality, the owners settled on a series of policies known as the reserve system.

The reserve system was another monopoly, this one on player talent. In adopting it, the owners took for themselves the right to decide where each player was to be allowed to ply his skills. From now on, when a player signed a contract with a club, he would go "on reserve," meaning he would "belong" to that club for as long as the club wanted him. He would be the club's property, property that could be sent out to play or kept on the bench, traded in exchange for another player, or sold for cash. Signing, a player forfeited his chance to make a better deal for himself with another team, as Boston's Spalding had done with Chicago the year before. Yet the way the owners had arranged matters, a player had no alternative *but* to sign. The rule was that no one without a contract might play on an NL team. A player who broke the rule faced discipline from the league as a whole.

As members of a cartel, NL teams did arrive at roughly equal strength. What was more, the reserve system finally put an end to interclub player raids. How? By providing that the clubs themselves, as well as individual players, could be disciplined for doing anything that threatened to undermine the reserve system. Furthermore, since a player had to agree to whatever terms his club offered—or quit the game—the reserve system benefited owners by allowing them to keep salaries lower than they would otherwise have been able to do. Overall, the owners' monopolistic practices gave them almost total control of their product: its quality, its availability, its cost. In one daring stroke, they had taken an activity that was all about competition and stripped it of just about every scrap of commercial competitiveness. Big-league baseball— big-league *sport*—was set to enjoy its first great boom.

Chapter 3

Money Matters

The National League of Professional Baseball Clubs was designed to make money, and it did. For some associated with the league, though, the money came in more quickly than for others. Among baseball's earliest millionaires was Albert Spalding.

There had been a good reason for Spalding's decision to jump from Boston to Chicago and from the old Players' Association to the new owners' league. Good reason, too, for him, a player, to have backed the monopolistic practices that were methodically reducing players to the level of bits of property. Only twenty-five years old in 1876, Spalding already seemed more of a baseball tycoon than a baseball player. Not only did he pitch for the Chicago White Stockings that year, he also managed the team, guiding it to a league-leading 52-14 finish. In addition, Spalding, Harry Wright, and a couple of others found the time—and money, $800—to open a sporting goods emporium in downtown Chicago.

It was the store that enabled Spalding to make his fortune. Or rather, it was the way he combined his roles as manager and merchant that made his fortune for him. As the manager of the White Stockings, Spalding ordered team members to wear uniforms out of his own stock. Since players had to pay for their uniforms themselves (at a cost to each of $30 a year), this decree meant quick profits for the young entrepreneur. More profit came in the form of an official monopoly under which the National League required all eight of its clubs to use Spalding baseballs. Spalding's company did not benefit directly under this arrangement since it supplied the balls to NL teams free of charge. However, the sight of professionals playing with top-grade, hand-sewn balls from Spalding's store inspired thousands of amateur players around the country to equip themselves with the mass-produced version of the real thing—also available from Spalding. Still more profit flowed from Spalding's exclusive right, again bestowed by monopoly-minded team owners, to print and sell the *Official Base Ball Guide*, a periodic compilation of statistics, records, rules, and anecdotes related to league activity.

Besides winning monopolies at the consumer end of his business empire, Spalding secured them at the supply end. He didn't just sell sporting goods, he manufactured them, taking care to keep production as smooth-running as possible. After an unexpected surge in the demand for baseball bats had once forced him to buy up old wagon parts to be reworked for the purpose, he bought a Michigan lumber mill, a cheap and ready source of wood.

Even as a captain of industry, Spalding remained active in NL affairs. In 1888–89, hoping to see baseball—and a call for its equipment—spread outside the United States, he conducted two teams on a $50,000, round-the-world exhibition tour. Except in Australia, the trip aroused little enthusiasm. Spalding did succeed in helping to gain acceptance for the myth—and myth it is, "cut from whole cloth," as Allen Guttmann puts it—that Abner Doubleday invented baseball one summer's day in 1839 in rural Cooperstown, New York. The fact that the U.S. national pastime was in reality a town sport derived from the English game of rounders offended Spalding's sense of patriotism and his nostalgic view of a bucolic American past.

If the National League was good for suppliers like Albert Spalding, it also proved profitable for team owners. Although league officials kept no attendance records in those early years, news accounts of the day suggest that fewer than 350,000 men, women, and children paid to watch baseball in 1876. Only the most successful clubs—Boston, with 64,550 home attendance, and Chicago, with 82,000—made money that year. (Because profit-and-loss figures can be computed in various ways, some sources show the Boston franchise losing money in its first season.) The next year, Chicago was the league's sole money-maker. St. Louis, its biggest loser, came up $6,000 short in 1877. The situation quickly improved. Gate receipts rose and so did profits. By the 1880s, teams were worth $7,000 and up, and in 1895, the New York Giants sold for an estimated $50,000. The NL had been just the ticket for transforming a common ordinary game into a modern sports enterprise.

So it was that when basketball was invented—the first game was played on December 21, 1891—no one had to ask how to organize the sport in order to profit from it. The answer was obvious. Select a limited number of the best teams. Form them into a league with strong central authority. Grant each team a territorial monopoly, and let owners determine player salaries and manage their clubs as each saw fit. Institute some form of a reserve system to prevent players from skipping from team to team, upping salaries and perhaps unbalancing overall league strength. Write common rules, draw up an acceptable schedule, set ticket prices, and hire referees. Sponsor play-offs to spark fan interest. Then sit back and enjoy success.

The plan worked. Not for basketball the decades-long progression from unruly folk game to village pastime to gentleman's leisure activity to commercial undertaking. Basketball was an immediate success on the college level, where territorial monopolies and the reserving of players to a particular team were automatic and salaries not an issue. On the professional level, the sport's first team was the Buffalo Germans, which began play in 1895. In 1898, a six-team pro basketball league was established. Although that league lasted only a few seasons, its place was taken by others. The American Basketball League, organized in 1925, was reorganized eight years later. The National Basketball League (NBL) appeared in 1937 and the Basketball Association of America (BAA) in 1946. In 1949, the NBL and the BAA joined to form today's National Basketball Association.

League bureaucracy worked in other professional team sports. The first pro ice hockey league came along in 1904; the present National Hockey League dates from 1917. Professional football got its start with a game played in Pennsylvania in 1895. The American Professional Football Association, set up in 1920, was renamed the National Football League two years later. Over the years, various other competing football leagues popped up. In 1970, the two-conference National Football League assumed its current form.

The league format—or variations on it—also turned out to work in nonprofessional sports. For the players who began contending at the revived Olympic Games in 1896 the league-like central authority was to be the International Olympic Committee (IOC). The IOC's job is to authorize events, plan schedules, arrange for facilities, set eligibility standards for participating athletes, and the like. Each competing country's Olympic team is managed by a national organization, such as the U.S. Olympic Committee (USOC). School and college sports are similarly organized along the lines of the baseball prototype. For U.S. college sports, the dominant "league" is the National Collegiate Athletic Association (NCAA). Formed in 1906, the NCAA now counts over 800 schools as members.

Even in most nonteam sports, the league plan dominates. An exception is boxing. *The World Almanac* lists five separate international boxing organizations in addition to the U.S. Boxing Association. Only in the heavyweight and lightweight divisions did even three of the six recognize the same champions. American boxing is licensed by the individual states, with scheduling, financing, and other arrangements left to individual promoters and managers. Horse racing is another state-licensed sport and decisions relating to it lie with track and racehorse owners, overseen by nationally organized racing groups.

For other sports, various federations or associations—the Professional Bowling Association, the National Association of Stock Car Auto Racing, the International Game Fish Association—play the central organizing role. The league plan also dominates tennis and golf. Both are governed by international federations with national groups, the U.S. Lawn Tennis Association (founded in 1881) and now known simply as the U.S. Tennis Association (USTA) and the American Professional Golfers Association (1916), functioning within the broader framework. These associations have real power over athletes, just as the original National League had power over its individual baseball players. In 1990, for example, the Ladies PGA declared Japan's top woman golfer, Ayako Okamoto, ineligible for a major tournament because she had accidentally neglected to initial her entry form. Earlier that year, on the other hand, the USTA did allow Jennifer Capriati to play in its U.S. Open, although under association rules the teenager was technically too young to compete. In each case, the "league" decision was respected by the athlete involved as well as by her manager, trainer, and advisers *and* by her competitors and *their* support groups. Everyone else involved in the event respected it, too. League authority—like the league itself or its equivalent—is fundamental to the business of modern sport.

Which is remarkable, since leagues, or rather, the monopolistic arrangements through which leagues tend to operate, are actually illegal in this country. And they have been since 1890, when the U.S. Congress passed the Sherman Antitrust Act.

That law, named for its chief sponsor, Ohio senator John Sherman, prohibited the making of any commercial arrangement aimed at setting prices, limiting production, assigning territorial markets, or barring competition. Ending competition, imposing territorial restrictions, rationing production, and fixing prices was of course what the National League of Professional Baseball Clubs was all about. Lucky for NL team owners that they organized their league before Sherman's bill cleared Congress.

Even luckier for them that the new law was for decades held not to apply to baseball anyway. Besides forbidding the formation of new trusts, the Sherman Act gave the U.S. government the power to break up old ones. Over the years, federal authorities have used this provision to dissolve a number of monopoly businesses, separating each into several smaller competing companies. The baseball cartel, however, remained for almost a century immune to any and all "trust busters." Why? Mostly because of the game's enormous popularity among Americans—including Americans in Congress and on the nation's courts of law. Thanks to their fondness for baseball, it—and, to a lesser degree, other sports—was allowed to retain certain unique monopoly privileges.

That is not to say that sports monopolies have gone unchallenged. During its first quarter century alone, baseball's NL faced threats from several would-be rivals. One of the most serious came in 1890 from a group calling itself the Players League.

As its name suggests, the new league was formed by team members hoping to regain control of their game and get rid of the hated reserve system, forcing NL owners to begin competing for players. Temporarily, the scheme worked. In 1889, the year before the Players League began offering contracts, a typical NL season's paycheck was $2,025. With the new league looking to fill its lineup slots and ready to raid National League clubs, that figure jumped 45 percent to $2,900. But after only two years, the inadequately financed Players League collapsed. Competition for players ended and the reserved system clicked back into place. The typical NL player salary plunged to $1,800 a year, $225 below what it had been in 1889.

The next real challenge to the NL monopoly came in 1901, when the minor-league American Association declared itself a major-league outfit with teams in eight cities, including some already hosting NL franchises. The upstart league's move was well timed, coming just as the NL was being weakened by quarrels and bickering among team owners. In addition to taking on the NL's territorial monopoly, the American League (AL) struck at its reserve system with a succession of generous salary offers. In its first year, the AL "stole" one hundred NL players. Its attack continued in 1902—only to be greeted by a counterattack on the part of NL owners willing to raise salaries if that was what it would take to win their players back. But although NL owners were too strong to succumb to the AL onslaught, they were not strong—or rich—enough to crush it once and for all. Peaceful coexistence seemed the only way out of the expensive mess.

In 1903, therefore, owners on both sides got together and agreed to a system of sixteen teams in two leagues, bound by common rules and nonconflicting schedules. They pledged to respect each other's territorial rights and reserve systems, eliminating the competition for fans and putting an end to that costly clubhouse piracy. Finally, the ingenious owners turned their rivalry to advantage by announcing a spectacular new championship sporting event, the World Series of Baseball. Never mind that their particular "world" extended only from Boston to St. Louis; it was the idea that counted, and this idea, the owners hoped, would sprout into an annual sports classic. It did. Except in 1904 when no play-off was scheduled, nothing has been known to stop the World Series— not war, not national crisis, not even, in 1989, an earthquake that shook San Francisco as its Giants prepared to take on the Oakland Athletics in game three of the championship. After a ten-day break devoted to fixing quake damage, Oakland went on to sweep the Series.

Along with pulling in a huge new national audience, the World Series served baseball indirectly by convincing team owners that there was more to running a successful sports business than establishing monopolies and clamping a lid on player salaries. As 1919's notorious Series demonstrated, they also had to take responsibility for keeping the game honest.

In the 1919 Series, the AL's overpoweringly superior Chicago White Sox lost to the NL's much weaker Cincinnati club. At first, fans were bewildered by Chicago's unexpectedly poor showing, but soon they learned the awful truth. The White Sox had deliberately played to lose. Several of the team's top stars had accepted bribes, cash payments from professional gamblers who made a bundle of their own by betting heavily on underdog Cincinnati.

The "Black Sox" affair not only darkened professional baseball's reputation, it threatened its very being. As the failure of the old National Association play-offs of the early 1870s had proved, the key to profit in commercial sport is exciting contests whose outcomes are in real, serious doubt. If that element of uncertainty is missing because of a betting fix, a chronic lack of balance among teams, or for any other reason, fans will lose interest in the competition. Owners in the two leagues knew they must act promptly to insulate their game from gamblers. Hastily, they hired a commissioner of baseball to help them police the sport.

Hastily but reluctantly, since the owners were unhappy at the thought of sharing their game with anyone. And having a commissioner did imply sharing. As the owners envisioned it, the commissioner would be responsible for seeing to it that everyone associated with professional baseball acted "in the best interests of" the sport. "Everyone" meant players, managers, scorekeepers, umpires, coaches—and owners. Naturally, owners balked at the idea of paying a salary to someone whose job it would be to keep an eye on them along with the hired help. At the same time, they recognized that to survive, baseball needed someone at the top to guarantee its integrity. It didn't take them long to conclude that a game shared with a commissioner was better than no game at all. Similar conclusions were reached by organizers in other sports, and as those organizers adopted or modified baseball's league plan they, too, provided for the post of commissioner or its equivalent.

Baseball's first commissioner, a former federal judge named Kenesaw Mountain Landis, lost no time in punishing the Black Sox for their misdeeds. He declared eight members of the team guilty of conspiring to throw the Series (though they had been found innocent in court) and banned them from the sport for life. Baseball was back on track and gathering steam for a new boom, a boom fueled only in part by Commissioner Landis's firm leadership. More fuel came from the U.S. Supreme Court, the nation's highest court of law, and its decision in the Federal League case.

The Federal League represented the third major challenge to the professional baseball monopoly. The Federal League was neither a players' group nor a stronger-than-average minor-league operation. It was a business proposition pure and simple, an ambitious attempt to cash in on baseball's swelling popularity. The new league had played through the 1914 and 1915 seasons, and once again, competition put baseball salaries on an upward track. American League outfielder Ty Cobb, still today the all-time major-league batting champ with a .367 lifetime average (meaning he averaged precisely 3.67 hits for every ten times at bat), saw his yearly income rise from $12,000 to $20,000 during the Federal League's brief existence. The paycheck of fastball hurler Walter Johnson, never yet surpassed in shutout games pitched, went from $7,000 to the same $20,000. But AL and NL owners were not about to spend that sort of money indefinitely; 1914 was the year the Boston Braves turned down as too expensive the opportunity to acquire two players—one of them rookie George Herman "Babe" Ruth—for $16,000. Nor were owners feuding as they had been in the NL when the AL had made its successful move fourteen years earlier. Fighting back with all the monopoly weapons at their disposal, the owners hung on to their markets, overwhelmed the Federals at the box office, and watched, gratified, as the rival league disintegrated.

Still set on tapping the baseball market, the Federal League partners sued, claiming that unfair violations of the Sherman Antitrust Act had forced them out of business. The suit eventually reached the Supreme Court.

The court handed down its decision in 1922, finding against the Federals and upholding baseball's monopoly status. Justice Oliver Wendell Holmes, writing for the majority, outlined the court's reasoning. Baseball, he asserted, is not a business in the sense of the Sherman Act. It is an "exhibition." Besides, federal antitrust legislation covers only activity that takes place across state lines. Trade within each state is a matter for state lawmakers, not the U.S. Congress. Since each game is played within a single state, Holmes concluded, measures regulating interstate commerce would not apply to baseball even if it were a real business.

It doesn't take a legal genius to spot flaws in that argument. Professional baseball games may be entertaining, but they are staged in the interests of selling tickets and making money. Big-league franchises are located in many different states, and teams cross state lines over and over in the course of a season. Furthermore, in years to come, the Supreme Court would rule that other entertainment industries—motion pictures, for example—were subject to federal antitrust laws despite the fact that they, too, involved exhibitions in separate locales within state borders. Even other sports such as football and basketball, although permitted in many ways to operate as monopolies, were never granted the sweeping antitrust exemptions awarded to baseball in 1922. The justices who decided *Federal League,* it seems, were no less sentimental about the game than Albert Spalding had been when he helped concoct the Abner Doubleday version of its origins.

Buoyed by its *Federal League* victory, and with the Black Sox scandal now behind it, baseball flourished. Large new parks, like New York's Yankee Stadium, were built to house the sport. Season attendance figures reached, and topped, the one million mark. So did the yearly dollar income from ticket sales. Other profits flowed into team owners' pockets—money from the sale of souvenirs and programs and from renting food sale rights to concessionaires and selling in-park billboard space to advertisers.

Other sports flourished along with baseball. Professional hockey and basketball leagues had achieved at least marginal success by the 1920s. Basketball had ranked as a major college sport for years. So had football, university presidents having gotten over their initial distaste for the game at the sight of the crowds flooding into their stadiums. Professional football was slower to catch on. The first pro team had appeared in 1895, but no really successful one emerged until 1919. That year, a businessman in Green Bay, Wisconsin, gave a local football club $500 to buy sweaters and stockings. In return, the benefactor asked only that each sweater bear the name of his business: the Indian Packing Company.

As team member and company employee Earl "Curly" Lambeau recalled, making money was not the point for the original Green Bay Packers. "We played for the love of the game. We agreed to split any money we got and each man was to pay his own doctor bills." The money came out of a hat passed among the spectators who stood around weekly behind a local brewery watching games. That first year, each regular Green Bay player got $16.75 for the season. Next year, arrangements were formalized. Lambeau's father, a carpenter, built bleachers alongside the playing field and enclosed both with a fence. It cost fans 50¢ to go beyond the fence.

Yet despite the new pay-to-watch policy, lack of money continued to be a problem for professional football. The league was struggling. Teams in some cities failed over and over, and in 1925 the value of the New York franchise was set at a mere $500. But if Timothy Mara, who took on the franchise at that price, thought he was getting a bargain, he was disappointed. Within months, Mara's expenses had passed $40,000. What football needed, he and other investors decided, was a star on the order of Babe Ruth or Ty Cobb to pull in the throngs. They looked around and there, just finishing his senior year at the University of Illinois, was the sensational halfback Harold "Red" Grange.

After a spirited competition among football owners, Grange signed with the Chicago Bears. His first day of play saw a 36,000-seat sellout at Wrigley Field, home of baseball's Chicago Cubs. (In those days, football teams were often compelled to borrow facilities—or rent them at up to $1,000 a game—from the richer sport.) The sellout was, says sportswriter Joseph Durso, "probably the first . . . ever drawn by pro football." It netted a $14,000 profit. Football was on its way.

So was golf. In 1895, the total purse for the game's U.S. championship was $335. Purses stayed low until players organized as pros, and even after the Professional Golfers Association came into being in 1916, many golfers continued to compete as amateurs. Bobby Jones, who won thirteen championship titles in England and America during the 1920s, never earned a cent on the course. But just four years after Jones retired in 1930, the new U.S. champion, Paul Runyan, took home almost $7,000. The money stakes were rising in horse racing as well. Overall, U.S. track purses went from just under $3 million a year in 1910, to well over $7 million ten years later, to nearly $14 million in 1930.

Yet over the next decade, horse racing purses climbed only another $2 million or so. Pro golfers found their cash rewards leveling out, too. Football also experienced lean times, NFL teams sometimes playing before a couple of thousand fans— and twenty times as many empty seats. In fact, it was lean times all around in the 1930s, the years of the Great Depression.

The depression had started in 1929 with the collapse of the New York stock market. The stock market is where stocks, or shares, in the nation's business and financial institutions are bought and sold, and when it crashed, the economy went with it. Banks and businesses failed, and millions of people lost their jobs, their homes, and their life's savings. With little cash to spare, Americans could not afford stadium tickets or racetrack bets, and the sports business suffered. Although big-league baseball was too firmly entrenched to be seriously endangered, the American Basketball League fell apart two years into the depression and had to be formed all over again in 1933. Creative minds in pro football met the empty-seat problem head-on, splitting into two divisions to permit new crowd-pleasing championship rivalries. The National Hockey League engaged in some franchise shuffling. Yet through all the upheaval, and even if they couldn't make it out to the game, sports-loving Americans could still keep in touch with the action. All they had to do was switch on the radio.

Radio sports broadcasting was only a few years old when the Great Depression struck. And radio itself was almost brand-new in April 1921, when a Pittsburgh station carried the first live sports broadcast, a boxing match. After that, sportscasting caught on fast. A second fight was aired in July and a Pittsburgh Pirates–Philadelphia Phillies baseball game in August. Speedboat races were reported on-air, and on college campuses, teachers and students experimented with broadcasting football games in progress. In 1922, New York's WJY began reporting baseball scores every fifteen minutes, while in Chicago, auto racing fans were treated to a seven-hour report of that year's Indianapolis 500. In the fall, Americans around the country heard the first radio World Series. Sport was poised for a new boom, this one powered by broadcasting.

But the boom had to wait. In the 1920s, sports broadcasting was still in its trial stage. After the twenties came the depression-ridden thirties. Then came the 1940s and World War II. For four years, from 1941 to 1945, the country was preoccupied with fighting in Europe and the Pacific Ocean. But when peace came at last, it brought with it economic prosperity, increased leisure time for most Americans, and a greater-than-ever demand for sports entertainment. And now there was television.

Although NBC-TV had broken into sports with the 1939 broadcast of a college baseball game, regularly televised contests were a postwar phenomenon. Among the earliest were the home games of the University of Pennsylvania's mighty football team. In 1950, the Los Angeles Rams became the first pro football team to appear on the small screen. A St. Louis golf tournament was broadcast locally in 1947, and boxing quickly became a late-night TV staple. Americans tuned in to every contest and begged for more. Broadcasters were glad to oblige. Presenting a spectacle arranged and financed by someone else costs only a fraction of the money it takes to produce original programming. For broadcasters, the major expense of airing a sports event is the cost of buying—from the person or organization in a position to sell it—the exclusive right to televise the contest. And that expense, television executives found, was one that commercial advertisers were delighted to cover—more than cover. As advertisers rushed to outbid each other for airtime during games, broadcasters realized they had stumbled upon a regular gold mine.

Less happy with the early broadcast picture were the nation's sports entrepreneurs. Would fans buy tickets to attend an event they could watch without cost at home? they wondered. Fight traffic and pay parking fees rather than enjoy a hassle-free afternoon in front of the TV? Trade living room comforts for the heat, cold, or rain of a stadium? The questions were especially worrisome in pro football, where the empty seats of the thirties remained a haunting nightmare. "Our stadiums may have to be turned into studios," one coach fretted. Even in the better-established college game, the fear of half-filled stands could not be dismissed. Yet neither college presidents nor NFL owners were willing to give up their newfound source of income from the sale of television rights by abandoning the medium altogether. Instead, they adopted blackout rules.

Blackouts amounted to a new form of sport's old territorial monopolies. Under the NFL's blackout rule, games could be broadcast, but only outside a seventy-five-mile radius of where they were being played. Within that radius, no coverage. Teams could still sell the rights to their games to broadcasters, and broadcasters would still get their money—plus profit—back from advertisers, but fans who lived seventy-five miles or less from the home stadium would have to buy a ticket to the game or miss it altogether. For college play, the NCAA came up with a rule of its own: just one game to be broadcast each week and that one blacked out locally.

Since such rules were aimed at preserving monopolies, and since monopolies are illegal in the United States, the rules were tested. The University of Pennsylvania, for example, which had been televising all its home games, determined to ignore the NCAA blackout. Penn would go right on broadcasting as before, university officials insisted. But group discipline was swift, and even powerful Penn couldn't withstand it. Acting on NCAA orders, the school's scheduled opponents announced that unless Penn abandoned its independent broadcast plans, they would refuse to turn up for games. Penn caved in. Not until the 1980s did U.S. courts break up the NCAA's broadcasting monopoly. With that, the College Football Association (CFA) stepped in to handle college football television contracts.

The blackout faced challenges at the professional level as well. In 1952, the U.S. government attacked the NFL rule as an illegal restraint of trade under the Sherman Act. Alarmed NFL owners raised $200,000 to fight the action. It was money well spent. In 1953, a federal court found blackouts, and the full stadiums they were designed to ensure, essential to the game's survival. Still, the battle wasn't over, and during the next few years, other cases in other courts were decided in ways that suggested that blackouts and other monopolistic broadcasting arrangements might one day be declared illegal. So sport—not just football, but other sports as well—turned to Congress, which alone has the power to change its own antitrust laws, and asked it to do exactly that. Congress came through with a 1961 measure exempting pro football, hockey, basketball, and baseball leagues from the antitrust provisions that normally applied to television.

Now the money poured in. Total professional football broadcast revenues were $3.5 million in 1961. The next year, they leapt to $5.2 million. In 1971, they came to $45.6 million, with $1.7 million of that going to each of the NFL's then twenty-six teams. In 1993, thanks to the $3.6 billion television deal signed by NFL Commissioner Paul Tagliabue at the start of the decade, each of the league's twenty-eight teams expected to pull in $39 million from television rights alone. (The $39 million apiece figure dropped slightly after the NFL returned $28 million to the networks in recognition of a drop in advertising revenues.) By the 1980s, some college teams were earning as much as $600,000 per broadcast, and football powerhouse Notre Dame entered its 1991 season with a new five-year $38 million contract with NBC-TV. The contract was a controversial one; to get it, Notre Dame broke with the CFA. By the year 2010, one television sports analyst predicts, Notre Dame will be taking in $100 million annually from TV football. Because it is television and its advertisers that absorb the costs of broadcasting each event, those figures represent almost pure profit to clubs, leagues, and associations.

Television has sent profits soaring in other sports. As we saw in chapter one, CBS-TV gave major-league baseball $1.06 billion for rights to its 1990–94 seasons. The same network paid $1 billion more to air NCAA tournament basketball between 1991 and 1997, while ABC-TV signed a $600 million pact with the NBA to cover its 1990–94 seasons. Nonteam sports, too, have found cartel-style ways of mining television's riches. In 1964, the PGA stopped allowing broadcasters to negotiate separately for the rights to individual golf matches and substituted an arrangement that forced them to buy entire packages of tournaments at previously unheard of prices. By the 1990s, the USTA, which controls broadcasting rights to the U.S. Open, was deriving 80 percent of its annual income from that source. As for televised Olympic competition, CBS paid $50,000 to air fifteen hours' worth of events from the 1960 Winter Games. Broadcasting the 1992 Olympic winter schedule cost the network $243 million, while NBC had to come up with $401 million for rights to that year's more event-filled Summer Games.

The sudden infusion of such vast amounts of money into sports didn't just enrich the industry, it changed it. Some changes appeared at the top, among sports owners and entrepreneurs. In the early days, most owners were sports enthusiasts first and sports investors second, like the Green Bay packer who enjoyed football and wanted a little publicity for his business. Some owners were popular with their players and some were not—rent the video of the 1988 movie *Eight Men Out* to see why the Chicago "Black Sox" didn't mind cheating boss Charlie Comiskey out of his World Series championship. Still, pleasant or irascible, generous or greedy, most early owners were committed to the game and involved on a personal level with their teams.

Today's owners may be equally involved—or they may not—but in either case, they and other front-office people tend to act as corporate executives first and sports fans sec-

ond. Even owners with longstanding ties to a team—like football Giants co-owner Wellington Mara, who was nine years
old when his father, Tim, bought the club in 1925—hire sophisticated staffs to run their enterprises on a corporate basis.
Some owners *are* corporations. Baseball's Chicago Cubs belongs to the Tribune Company, a news outfit, and basketball's
New York Knicks to Paramount Communications, the movie
and publishing conglomerate.

The switch from a personal management style to a corporate one is tied to another change in sports: a change in the
reason that many owners become owners. Once, owners got
into the game because they wanted to be part of a sporting
venture. Today, they may also want a tax break.

The first break comes on the club itself. Professional sports
clubs, like other businesses, are required to pay a tax on their
income. (College teams, by contrast, are not taxed on their
direct income, since they belong to tax-exempt educational
institutions. The not-for-profit U.S. Olympic Committee also
enjoys tax-exempt status.) But owners of professional teams
do have to calculate their yearly earnings (from admissions,
concessions, advertising, the sale of broadcast rights, and so
on), and their expenses (salaries and wages, travel, equipment,
insurance, advertising, and publicity). If income is greater than
outgo, the owner pays tax. If it's less, no tax is due. In many
cases, says Benjamin A. Okner of the Brookings Institution, a
Washington, D.C., think tank, surprisingly little ends up with
the government.

One reason for that is that the law allows a new owner to
claim that the team begins decreasing in value the moment he
or she (or, in the case of a corporate owner, it) takes over.
Here's how the system works. When a team is bought, the
buyer pays, not just for the franchise itself—that is, for the
league-given right to play in a particular city—but also for

the contracts of team members. And each of those contracts is regarded as "depreciating," becoming worth less year by year as the player ages, getting closer to retirement and perhaps declining in strength and skill. The contracts' combined loss of value is a loss the new owner can use to offset profits, and that offset reduces the amount of tax owed. Sports clubs are unique, Okner says, in providing their owners with living tax write-offs. In other industries, owners can claim depreciation on equipment like trucks or computers, but only in sports are human workers considered to be physical properties that lose value over time.

Owners find other tax breaks beyond human depreciation. The biggest one may come from the team "losses" they write off against profits from their other corporate undertakings.

Most modern team owners do have other such undertakings—how else could they have afforded their clubs' multimillion-dollar price tags? Atlanta Braves owner Ted Turner's primary business is cable television. Texas Rangers co-owner George W. Bush is an oil developer and the son of former President Bush. But even team owners who are rich entrepreneurs, presidential sons, or corporations are expected to file tax returns. If, however, individual or corporate owners can show that while their nonsports businesses are thriving, their clubs are losing money, they can use the club loss to offset those nonsports profits. Again, the offset saves on taxes. Nor are sports losses hard to find—not for those looking for them. Remember that the 1876 Boston Red Stockings either made money or lost it, depending upon whose figures you believe. Anyone who really wants to will be able to find enough "paper losses" to satisfy tax collectors. Finding them is one of the tasks of the clever accountants and lawyers on those corporate club staffs.

Changes in sports ownership—and even more, changes behind the reasons for that ownership—go a long way toward explaining some of the other changes that have hit sports in recent years. They help explain, for instance, why clubs are bought and sold so frequently—thirteen NFL sales between 1981 and the end of 1991 alone. Player contracts can be depreciated only over a five-to-seven-year period. Once that time is up, the owner's tax saving disappears and his or her best financial bet may be to sell the team. Resale almost always means a profit, since potential new owners can look forward to a tax break of their own. If the sellers then turn around and buy new franchises, they can begin depreciating all over again.

This businesslike outlook on the part of ownership and management also helps account for the footloose ways of modern teams. Each of the sixteen baseball teams of the combined National and American leagues stayed put in its original city for half a century. Then, in 1953, the Boston Braves moved to Milwaukee with NL approval. A dozen years later, the Braves moved back east to Atlanta, a move dictated by corporate—financial—motives. Not only had Atlanta city officials agreed to pay $18 million to build the team a new stadium, but they also promised $1.2 million in local television revenues for 1966. (Although the league is in charge of national network broadcasting, teams negotiate their own local arrangements.) A stadium constructed at public expense plus $1.2 million? Who could resist it? Not the Braves, then making under a quarter million dollars a year out of Milwaukee television.

A lot of other teams couldn't resist either. Baseball's New York Giants found a spanking-new city-financed home in San Francisco. The Dodgers broke Brooklyn hearts with a move to Los Angeles. The Washington Redskins football team went to Minnesota, tripling its TV earnings in the process. The switches have continued and look as if they will go on into the future, with money ever the driving force. They're even occurring on the college level. The 1990s began with major shifts in college football and basketball conference alignments—the Southeast Conference raiding the Southwest Conference, for example, and the Big Ten turning into the Big Eleven—all in the interests of gaining new television markets.

Not only do the vast amounts to be made in sports keep propelling old clubs to new cities, they produce whole new clubs—whole new leagues even. Expansion has come in every team sport. In 1992, the NFL had twenty-eight teams, up from thirteen at the end of the 1960s. The NBA, ten teams strong in the mid-1970s, had twenty-seven clubs as the nineties began. The six-team NHL of the late seventies had grown to twenty-one franchises, with an additional two clubs scheduled to debut in time for the 1992–93 season. As of 1993, major-league baseball will have twenty-eight teams. Some of the new teams are the result of deliberate league planning, but others are evidence of the league crashing that began in 1960 with the American Football League (AFL).

The AFL's chief backer, Texas oilman Lamar Hunt, actually began with the intention of buying an existing NFL franchise. None was available. Then he tried to break into the league by creating a new NFL team of his own and ran smack up against impenetrable monopolies. So Hunt did what Joseph Durso calls "the only sensible thing . . . for a man who had inherited a couple of hundred million dollars." He found a few other rich investors and set up a new league with eight teams and a TV contract worth $1.78 million in its first year. Although the AFL was never a roaring success, its television revenues kept it alive long enough to become a thorn in the side of the NFL. In 1966, the older league gave in and agreed to a merger.

Hunt's victory sparked other league-crashing attempts. The World Football League was organized and played in 1974 and 1975 but was too weak financially to get the NFL even thinking about a second merger. The U.S. Football League, organized in 1982, failed three years later. The American Basketball Association, established in 1967 to break into the NBA, did better. In 1976, the NBA agreed to join with the ABA in a new monopoly. Three years later, the NHL was compelled to absorb the four surviving teams of the nine-year-old World Hockey Association (WHA) into its cartel.

By the 1990s, league expansion and creation had assumed international proportions. The Memphis-based World Basketball League (WBL), with teams in the United States, the Soviet Union, Australia, and Italy, among other countries, started operations in 1987. The NFL's World League of American Football began play in 1991 (and suspended it in 1992), and the NFL plans to add Canadian and English franchises to its own ranks by the end of the decade. Canada has an American-style football league, the Canadian Football League (CFL), as well. Baseball went international in 1969 with the NL's Montreal Expos, while hockey, Canadian in origin, has been a two-nation sport since the NHL's inception. Even leagues that are technically all-American are assuming an international flavor. The first regular-season game in any major-league U.S. sport played outside North America took place in 1990 in Japan between two NBA teams. NBA teams also meet European clubs in tournament play. Empty spots on U.S. high school and college basketball teams are increasingly being filled by players from Australia, Nigeria, Yugoslavia, Spain, and thirty or more other countries. Worldwide, it's estimated that 250 million people play in some organized basketball league program. By the same token, sports popular outside the United States are seeking American audiences.

The 1994 World Cup soccer championship series was scheduled to be played here, a prelude, soccer promoters hoped, to establishing the game big-time in this country. If American fans do take to soccer, it will be a bonanza for American television; one billion people around the globe watched the 1990 World Cup final, a figure that dwarfs that year's Super Bowl audience of about 100 million.

While all this team sport expansion was going in, nonteam sports were also growing explosively. Today's golfers and tennis players have busier schedules than ever before. Tennis used to center around Davis Cup competition and four annual Grand Slam events: the U.S. Open, the French Open, the Australian Open, and England's Wimbledon. Now there are more than seventy additional tournaments, all financed principally by television. In golf, the few classics of Bobby Jones's day have expanded into a nearly year-round schedule of televised play.

Not only are there more sports events than ever, each event attracts more competitors. Fifty-six players entered golf's first U.S. Open in 1895. Entrants today number in the hundreds, with thousands more trying and failing to win the chance to compete. The Senior PGA Tour was established in 1980 with two tournaments and $250,000 in prizes. By the nineties, it included thirty-seven tournaments and over $14 million in prizes. Tennis, too, began attracting large numbers of professionals as the television dollars flooded in, and the USTA does all it can to attract even more, spending $10 million a year on its junior development programs.

Television money feeds other sports. Horse racing dates have become more frequent. So have stock car races, track and field events, winter sports contests, bicycle races, footraces, and marathons. What's more, television has discovered sport where only games and recreation once existed: table tennis, bowling, championship rodeo, volleyball, rock climbing, truck and tractor mud-bogging. What will be next? "Tid-dlywinks?" pondered one of the men responsible for the WHA and the ABA. According to him, someone brought it up to him as a real TV sports possibility. "Truthfully," he says, "someone did."

If tiddlywinks does come to television, it's safe to say it won't arrive in its traditional form. For not only has television money created some new sports and financed the expansion of others, it has also changed sports themselves and the way they are played. One of the changes for which TV is responsible, some observers charge, is sport's increasing violence.

Are they right? It is certainly true that many sports are more violent now than in the past. Even in hockey and football, rough from the start, injuries are on the upswing. According to Allen Guttmann, 186 NFLers were on the injured reserve list at midseason in 1978. At the same point in 1986, 286 were listed. Basketball, invented as a noncontact sport, has its brawls, many of them bloody. So violent had the game become that before its 1990–91 season opened, the NBA announced harsher penalties for players who commit overly aggressive fouls. Tennis players, once the most decorous of athletes, hurl racquets and scream insults at fans and referees. Are TV cameras to blame for the mayhem? Former football defensive back Bernie Parrish thinks so, suggesting that players eager for television exposure may unnecessarily pile on in a tackle in order to get their names mentioned over the airwaves. Other players apparently figure that outrageous on-camera behavior makes them better known—and therefore more likely to be chosen to endorse commercial products. "With his trademark bad manners," says *Forbes* magazine, tennis star Andre Agassi "has become a celebrity." "Bad manners" being a euphemism for interrupting a match to smash to bits not one, but two, racquets. And, *Forbes* continues,

"Celebrity means money . . . Nike has just re-signed Agassi, tantrums and all, to an estimated $2 million-a-year contract."

Whether or not television contributes to sports violence, it is clearly responsible for another change: growing specialization. Specialization is characteristic of modern sport, and television, Richard Mandell contends, only makes it more so. With its close-up shots, numerous camera angles, slow motion, and instant replays, television encourages athletes to concentrate on precision in one small area of play instead of working to develop overall ability. "A consequence of this," says Mandell, "has been to allow increasingly the substitution of skilled player 'specialists' with specific roles . . . Examples are designated hitters in baseball and place kickers in football." Football's platoon system—one team for offense, a different one for defense—is another symptom of the movement toward specialization. Ironically, as some see it, the trend may be doing as much to reduce player skill as to enhance it. The steady stream of substitutes, complains retired Oakland Raider Ken Stabler, means that quarterbacks no longer have to be as crafty as they were in the past. Stabler would like to turn the clock back on that one. He also wanted the League to do away with second-guessing instant replay, another television contribution. "I'd like to see the game put back into the officials' hands," Stabler said in 1990. "Let them call it." Fifteen months later, the NFL did put an end to its six-year experiment with instant replay.

Commercial television has meant other changes. U.S. tennis officials increased the pace of their game and pleased broadcast executives by adopting the tie-breaker rule in 1970. Pro football went along with the demands of television advertisers and agreed to allow network employees to call some time outs, planning them around ad schedules. "The game is now run upstairs in the booth and funneled down to the coach or the offensive coordinator," Ken Stabler remarks. He doesn't like that. Some fans echo Stabler's objections to letting TV call the shots on the field—but at least the practice lets viewers enjoy all the action. Tennis fans aren't so fortunate; as one griped in a letter to the *New York Times,* "Long commercials lead to the next point often being missed."

The NFL made another concession to TV's commercial demands at the start of the 1990–91 season, cutting halftimes from fifteen minutes to twelve and allowing the clock to be restarted more quickly after a play goes out of bounds. Players weren't thrilled by the change, which threatened to reduce the number of plays per game from sixty to forty and left team members with only about six minutes to catch their breath during halftime, but broadcasters insisted upon it. Under the new rules, the average contest lasts only two hours and fifty-two minutes as opposed to three hours and seven minutes. That fifteen-minute time saving keeps afternoon games from running over into television's profitable prime-time evening schedules.

Television has even changed the timing of sports seasons. Anxious to milk the medium for everything they can, sports people have extended their schedules, donned warmer uniforms—or lighter-weight ones—and taken refuge in domed stadiums and on artificial grass. "Pro football," says James Reston, sports fan and former columnist and editor at the *New York Times,* "which is a cool-weather game, now starts in August. Pro baseball, which is a hot-weather game, now starts in the cold and rain of the capricious spring. Pro basketball, which is an indoor winter sport, now runs from late summer to May. Everybody is out for the Big Buck and the television contracts are king."

If the contracts are king, all else is secondary—even sport itself. So it was that when CBS-TV looked at its 1990 World

Series and league play-off schedule and saw a problem, baseball, in the person of Fay Vincent, commissioner from 1989 to 1992, hastened to fix it.

The problem lay with the National League play-offs, in which the Pittsburgh Pirates and Cincinnati Reds were to face each other on Thursday and Friday, October 4 and 5. Saturday would normally have been a day off, with the third game to be played on Sunday. But a Sunday game would have conflicted with CBS college football coverage and the network's commitment to the AL play-offs. So the third Pirates–Reds game was postponed until Monday. Monday afternoon, since a night game would have had to compete for its TV audience with Monday Night Football. The Pirates couldn't even hold weekend workouts in their own home stadium since its field was set up for Sunday's Pittsburgh Steelers football game.

"That's not normal," says *New York Times* sports reporter Dave Anderson. To perform at their best, athletes need to practice and stick to a regular schedule. But in modern consumer sports, athletics isn't the point; advertising dollars are. "Such is life," Anderson wrote, "when the television tail wags the baseball dog." As Commissioner Vincent explained his decision to postpone the Pittsburgh-Cincinnati game, "We have to make accommodations to business realities." What "realities"? The $270 million CBS had paid major-league baseball for a package that included the NL play-offs. "This is ultimately a business," Vincent pointed out.

It sure is. Sports is a business that has been making money— plenty of money—for its capital investors since Albert Spalding and his friends came up with their league plan in 1876. Only now, thanks to some trustbusting that began in the 1970s and continues today, is the sports business making plenty for its workers as well.

Chapter 4

Those "Greedy" Players

Poor Rickey Henderson. Baseball's salary king at $3 million a year for a brief glorious moment in 1989, Henderson had seen himself almost instantly dethroned by the likes of Don Mattingly, Will Clark, Dave Stewart, and, most hurtfully of all, by Jose Canseco, the game's first $5 million-a-year player. Then had come Darryl Strawberry . . . Roger Clemens . . . Bobby Bonilla . . . By the time the 1992 season rolled around, Henderson no longer ranked even among baseball's top twenty-five in earnings.

And poor Scott Stevens. In July 1990, the St. Louis Blues had stunned the hockey world by making Stevens that game's highest-paid defensive player with a contract worth $775,000 in its first year. But just weeks later, the Boston Bruins handed defenseman Ray Bourque a new contract for $1.1 million a year—at a time when Bourque's old contract, under which he was getting less than Stevens, hadn't yet expired. The Bruins had torn up a perfectly valid document simply to keep Bourque happy.

Was Bourque happy though? How must he have felt after Wayne Gretzky struck his $31 million ten-year deal with the Los Angeles Kings? What was his million-odd compared to that?

How, come to that, must the New York Knicks' Patrick

Ewing, best-paid in the NBA at about $4 million in 1990–91, have felt when the Cleveland Cavaliers put forward John "Hot Rod" Williams ahead of him at $5 million a year? How must *Williams* have reacted when Ewing reestablished his salary lead with a $33 million six-year contract? Then there was Boris Becker. Becker began the 1990s as the world's highest-paid tennis player, but before the decade's first year was out he had seen nineteen-year-old Pete Sampras win a brand-new tennis event, the Grand Slam Cup, in twelve sets to earn $2 million—twice as much as any tennis player had ever before won in a single match. "Perverse," said Becker.

Others would use stronger language. Take Bruins general manager Harry Sinden. It was Sinden who did the rewriting on Ray Bourque's contract, a fact he wasn't happy about. "I'm really disgusted with myself," he told reporters. "I got in a situation created by other people and I had to capitulate. I'm talking about what St. Louis did [for Stevens]." Sinden didn't like raising Bourque's pay ahead of schedule, but figured he had to or risk losing the star to a better deal in a different city.

Or how about a hockey club president like the Vancouver Canucks' Pat Quinn, the man who, as we saw in chapter one, called the St. Louis offer to Stevens "frightening"? Of course, Quinn found it frightening. Once teams start bidding against each other for players' services, salaries spiral. It was to keep any wage spiral from ever starting in baseball that the NL had instituted its reserve system in the 1870s. That system, upheld by the U.S. Supreme Court in 1922, found renewed court backing in 1953. And it was to keep profit-lowering salary spirals out of other sports that teams in other leagues had adopted their own systems for monopolizing players. Generally speaking, those systems required players to sign contracts giving their club the option of signing them again the next year. Football's and basketball's option systems were never quite as inflexible as baseball's reserve system, since a player could theoretically "play out his option," then go on to negotiate with another team. Still, since it was in each team's interest to keep players from going from club to club—at higher and higher wages—most owners were wary of being too generous with anyone who did exercise his right to look for a new team. In football, a rule handed down by Alvin "Pete" Rozelle, commissioner from 1959 to 1989, further discouraged team-to-team movement and consequent salary competition. Under the Rozelle Rule, any team that acquired someone who had played out his option with another club was obliged to recompense the player's old club either in cash or with other players. Even now the National Hockey League operates under a Rozelle-type rule that makes hockey clubs reluctant to pursue stars with generous salary offers. Later on in this chapter we'll see how the NHL rule affects players today.

Sport's reserve systems were naturally unpopular with athletes. Football, basketball, and hockey players didn't like the restraints placed on their movements any more than baseball players did, and no one liked the skimpy salaries that, except in the case of a few well-paid superstars, went along with them. Television and its advertisers were pouring more and more money into league and club offices, and it seemed to players that since they were the ones who were attracting the viewers—and with them, the advertising—they deserved a bigger cut of the total. Nonteam athletes were also seeing huge sums going to their leaguelike central organizations, and they, too, felt they were being denied their fair share. Throughout sport, player rebellions simmered.

But the rebellions were fitful at first and changes a long time coming. In 1954, perhaps remembering Albert Spalding's comment about the division between capital and labor, baseball players organized the Major League Ball Players Association (MLBPA). Not until the mid-1960s, though, did the group begin acting like a real labor union. Then, under the tough-minded leadership of a former official of the United Steelworkers Union named Marvin Miller, the MLBPA demanded—and got—such basic worker benefits as medical insurance and pensions. One significant MLBPA victory came in 1968 when baseball owners accepted a system of arbitration that gave some unhappy players the right to have their contract grievances heard and judged by an impartial mediator.

Meantime, athletes in other sports were engaging in their own battles—and realizing a few victories. In 1955, the Supreme Court found against a New York firm accused of trying to monopolize U.S. boxing. Two years later, the Court declared it a violation of antitrust statutes for professional football to "blacklist" a player—that is, to discipline him for infractions of league rules by refusing to allow him to play on any NFL club. In 1967, three years after the PGA multiplied its television profits by forcing broadcasters to buy golf by the package, some pros refused to play until a greater percentage of those profits found their way out of association bank accounts and into tournament purses. It took a year, but the "strikers" won their point. Next year, the USLTA succumbed to pressure from professional tennis players and agreed to allow them into its amateur contests, older and more prestigious than professional ones. Fans were delighted by the new combination of the most outstanding events and the most skilled players, and "open" tennis turned into a game of megabucks. In 1972, tennis players eager to consolidate their gains formed their own union, the Association of Tennis Professionals (ATP). But if 1972 was a good year for tennis pros, it was a disastrous one for baseball players. Once again, the Supreme Court ruled in favor of the reserve system.

The ruling came in the case of Curt Flood, a center fielder

trying to get out of his contract with the St. Louis Cardinals. As far as the court was concerned, Flood's contract was, like the reserve system itself, binding. Although that system was an "aberration," Justice Harry A. Blackmun wrote for the majority, it had been around so long, and was so firmly established, that it would be unfair for the court to upset it now. Not just unfair, Blackmun implied, almost un-American. Much of his opinion consisted of a lyrical tribute to the game of baseball, a tribute that invoked eighty-eight of its greats by name. "The list seems endless," the Justice observed, and went on to quote from "Casey at the Bat" by Ernest L. Thayer. In this comic 1888 poem, the mighty Casey, pride of the Mudville baseball team, swings at, and misses, an all-important third-strike pitch. Blackmun's drift was clear: like the ill-fated Casey, Flood was about to strike out. If, however, *Congress* wanted to apply antitrust law to baseball, it should do so.

Congress declined Blackmun's invitation, but the reserve system proved to be doomed anyway. In 1975, players Andy Messersmith and Dave McNally went to arbitration, asking to be released from their clubs. The two won their case. Baseball owners, confident in their 1972 Supreme Court triumph, sued—and were dismayed to lose at the district court level. Could they expect higher courts to save their "aberration" yet again? Suspecting that the answer was "No," and fearing that if they pursued their fight the reserve system would be taken from them altogether, the owners agreed to a compromise. From now on, and under certain conditions, players with several years' experience in the majors (six then, five today) would be free to negotiate with a number of different clubs. In 1976, baseball's first free agents hit the market. After a century of trying, players had cracked sport's oldest reserve system. Simultaneously, similar systems in other sports, less secure under the law than baseball's to begin with, crumbled as well.

So it was that sport became a money game on the bench as well as in the front office. No need to review those breathtaking salaries and purses; every sports fan is familiar with their bulk and heft. Familiar, too, with the fact that professional athletes are as determined as employees in any other field to keep their paychecks high, working conditions good, and pension, health care, and other benefits on the rise. What's more, like laborers in other industries, men and women in sports are willing to resort to whatever tactics seem necessary to turn that determination into reality. The 1981 baseball season was interrupted by a strike that lasted from June 12 to August 10. NFL players walked out for eight weeks in 1982. Five years later, another NFL strike led to a relaxation of the Rozelle Rule and an easier path to free agency. A brief hockey players' strike for a time threatened to cancel the NHL's 1992 Stanley Cup championship play-off series.

Athletes, following the example of movie stars and others in the entertainment world, engage professional agents, lawyers, and financial advisers to represent them and work out the best possible contracts. Football players like Lawrence Taylor sit out days or weeks of training camp, waiting for sweeter deals to emerge from management. Basketball stars— the Boston Celtics's guard Brian Shaw was one example— desert their team, even their country, for megasalaries with a European club.

Sometimes, the determination to win in the money game turns nasty. In the late 1980s, the International Tennis Association and the Association of Tennis Professionals began a struggle for control of the sport and its profits. According to estimates (since the ITA is a private organization, its financial records may be kept confidential), players were getting in prizes only about a fifth of the money the ITA and its national member associations were taking in each year from their four Grand Slams, the Davis Cup match, and some seventy other events. The ATP wanted more, and in 1990, it managed to wrest ownership of the game's non–Grand Slam and Davis Cup contests from the international group.

The ITA wasn't about to take that loss sitting still. Its response: invent a new match, label it the Grand Slam Cup, and "bribe"—*Sports Illustrated*'s word—top players to "betray"—*SI* again—their fellow ATP members by taking part in it. Nineteen ninety's bribe came to $6 million, of which Pete Sampras took one-third. It was the bribery aspect, as much as the $2 million itself, that prompted Boris Becker's "perverse." Becker refused to play in the Grand Slam Cup and so did some others, including Andre Agassi. Agassi, however, first pledged to appear, then withdrew, calling the event an ITA attempt "to deceive the world" into accepting a hastily constructed event as a classic tournament simply because of the size of its purse. Deception? Agassi's excuse for withdrawing was a torn cartilage. His claim to be hurt came under fire from the ITA after a California sportswriter reported overhearing Agassi and his brother wondering aloud where they could find a doctor willing to confirm the injury. That indiscretion cost Agassi a $25,000 ITA fine for dodging play.

Not all of sport's money games are so contentious. Not all involve on-field play, either. For some pro athletes, already earning millions from their sport, the really big money comes from commercial endorsement contracts.

Endorsement opportunities, so highly prized by athletes, seem like a good deal all-round. Good for manufacturers, assured that their products will be snapped up if only buyers can be persuaded that those products are also the choice of attractive, popular young stars. Good for the stars, who can earn millions by saying—probably truthfully—that they play with Prince racquets, drink Coke, depend on a particular brand of aspirin, and drop in at McDonald's. (Well, not always truthfully. Tennis great Jimmy Connors, who in 1982 signed an eleven-year contract with Converse sneakers, caused a stir by showing up at the 1991 U.S. Open in Nikes.) Product endorsements are even popular with those sports fans who get a kick out of seeing and hearing their favorites in offbeat or entertaining settings.

Still, endorsements have their downside. For fifteen-year-old Michael Thomas, just finishing ninth grade in a Maryland school in 1989, the downside was grim indeed. Michael, a basketball player and admirer of NBA star Michael Jordan, owned a $115.50 pair of Nike Air Jordans. According to his family, he treasured those sneakers, cleaning them daily and storing them in their original box with Jordan's image on the cover. "We told him not to wear the shoes to school," Michael's grandmother remembers. "We said somebody might like them, and he said, 'Granny, before I let anyone take those shoes, they'll have to kill me.'" They did. One spring day, Michael's strangled, shoeless body was found near his school. His killer: a fellow basketball player and Jordan fan.

Michael Thomas is not the only U.S. teenager to have died for his sports celebrity-endorsed sneakers. Between 1985 and 1989, at least six others suffered the same fate. More were murdered for other articles of sports clothing, jackets, caps, and sweatpants among them. Jackets are especially in demand; a New York boy was killed in a junior high school corridor for his Georgetown University jacket, and a Chicago nineteen-year-old was shot to death for refusing to surrender his Cincinnati Bengals jacket. Hundreds of youngsters have been beaten up and their clothing stolen. A Chicago police sergeant whose division covers just four of the city's twenty-five police districts reports handling over sixty violent incidents involving athletic shoes and clothing a month. The crimes disturb him, and not just because they involve law-breaking. "When you really think about the crime itself— taking someone's clothes off their body," he told *Sports Illustrated*, "you can't get much more basic." True, and as *SI*'s Rick Telander points out, the criminals aren't taking just clothes. "They're taking status."

The status they are taking along with the clothes is the status of the athlete who endorsed them. No endorsement, no status, and that raises the question: should athletes feel any responsibility if violence breaks out over products bearing their names? Michael Jordan seems to. Reporter Telander described him as being near tears as he read news accounts of Michael Thomas's death. But what was Jordan supposed to do? Stop endorsing the shoe that Nike developed expressly to bear his name?

Some might argue that he should. *Forbes* magazine showed Jordan earning a $2.1 million salary in 1990, while raking in another $6 million in endorsements. Wheaties, Coca-Cola, and McDonald's were all paying the Chicago Bulls star handsomely, and American kids weren't mugging and murdering other kids over cereals, soft drinks, and fast food. Couldn't the superrich Jordan afford to stop doing ads for one consumer item they do kill for?

Even leaving the violence aside, critics say, sports figures ought to be asking themselves other questions about some of their endorsements. Is it right to promote shoes costing as much as $170 a pair to teenagers? Even young people with paying jobs may not be able to afford such prices, and by no means all teens have jobs. Many of those toward whom basketball sneaker promotions are most directly addressed live in America's inner cities, where basketball is nearly a way of life. Many come from jobless or poverty-stricken families. Anyway, income aside, is it ethical to encourage materialism among people of any age or background by suggesting that it's what they *own* that makes them what they are?

Other critics express other reservations about athletes' commercial ties. What, for instance, about stars who, while not actually endorsing a product, nevertheless lend their names to it? This sort of passive promotion is nothing new. The original Green Bay Packers indulged in it, and so have countless others who, throughout the history of modern sport, have performed in front of billboards and signs advertising everything from razor blades to soft drinks to cars. But by the 1990s, simple "signage" had turned into an almost universal sponsorship of sport. Just glance at the morning sports pages. It's like reading a corporate directory: Chrysler, Nestlé, Bank of Boston, Shearson Lehman Hutton . . . But look closer: it's the Bob Hope Chrysler Classic, the Nestlé Invitational, the Bank of Boston Classic, and the Shearson Lehman Hutton Open—all golfing events. Auto racing has its Coca-Cola 600, its Pontiac Excitement 400, and its Banquet Frozen Foods 300; tennis, its Lipton and Volvo Internationals; professional bowling, its Tums Classic. College football teams that used to show up at the Cotton Bowl, Orange Bowl, and Independence Bowl now play at the Mobil Cotton Bowl, the Federal Express Orange Bowl, and the Poulan/Weed Eater Independence Bowl. The Sun Bowl has lost its identity altogether; in 1991 it was officially rechristened the John Hancock Bowl in honor of its insurance-company sponsor. Then there's the Virginia Slims tennis tour.

The Slims tour—along with the players who participate in it—is one that comes in for some special criticism. Why? Virginia Slims are cigarettes, and as such, says the American Lung Association, they contribute to some percentage of this country's 390,000 annual tobacco-related deaths. Should tennis players, who most certainly do not smoke themselves, tacitly encourage others to do so? Take Slims money, saying, in effect, "This product is okay by me. Go ahead. Use it"? Not by the standards of U.S. Secretary of the Department of Health and Human Services, Louis W. Sullivan. "Blood money," Sullivan called Virginia Slims purses in 1990, adding, "An athlete or sports figure should not allow his or her good name . . . to push a product that, when used as intended, causes death." But many do.

Others permit their names to be linked to various brands of beer. Three of the nation's biggest brewers, Miller, Anheuser-Busch, and Coors, spend $50 million a year to sponsor auto racing. Drivers and their vehicles, emblazoned with brand names and beer company logos, speed around the track at 170 mph and over. The clear message: hard drinking and fast driving do mix.

Beer companies don't limit their sports sponsorship to auto racing. Overall, Anheuser-Busch spent $175 million on sports events in 1990; Coors, another $53 million. Add to those amounts the money laid out by leading tobacco companies—Philip Morris, maker of Virginia Slims, spent $128 million on sport in 1990, and RJR Nabisco (Winston), $115 million—for a grand total of $471 million. That's close to half a billion dollars from just four companies, all of it going, directly or indirectly, to vigorous young athletes in peak condition who repay their benefactors by promoting products known to help cause disease and death. No wonder sports stars get such bad press. *Sports Illustrated* isn't alone in scorning the "filthy rich" among them. "For too many professional athletes," says Dave Anderson of the *New York Times,* the main career focus is "trying to make the most money." *Forbes* depicted athletes as "chas[ing] the bucks, no apologies."

Do they really need every last one of those bucks? What if rich athletes simply refused to cooperate with corporations that make and sell potentially harmful products? Just said no to invitations to appear at the matches and competitions they sponsor? After all, Boris Becker and Andre Agassi felt they could afford to boycott the ITA's 1990 Grand Slam Cup. So why can't others stay away from the Virginia Slims Tour or golf's Anheuser-Busch Classic? Of course, the Grand Slam Cup boycott was the result of what players saw as an ITA threat to their efforts to pick up a greater share of tennis income. A Virginia Slims boycott, on the other hand, would be a matter of pure principle. Can it be that athletes put money before principle?

A growing number of people suspect they do, and greed is only one of the faults sportswriters and others find in modern sports stars. Columnists are quick to characterize athletes as "cocky," "arrogant," or "obnoxious." Robert J. Kelleher of the *New York Times* called tennis players "crybabies" for complaining about off-court conditions at Grand Slam tournaments. *Forbes* dwelt lengthily on Agassi's "poor sportsmanship" and headlined a story about endorsement incomes "Throw a Tantrum, Sign a Contract."

Sometimes it seems that no matter what an athlete does, reporters are bound to react cynically. Early in the 1990–91 NBA season, the LA Lakers's Magic Johnson announced he was giving $100,000 of his $3.1 million salary back to the club so the Lakers could afford to acquire guard Terry Teagle. (Under NBA rules, no team is allowed to exceed a set amount— $11.8 million in 1990—in total player salaries.) Johnson's gesture inspired Jack McCallum of *SI* to satire. "The idea of rich and famous athletes giving back money is the best thing to come along in sports since arena pizza delivery," McCallum wrote. Why not "Give-Backs"—"G-Bs"—for all athletes? he suggested. Why not include G-B figures in a player's official statistics? Other writers take the snide approach. When baseball's Darryl Strawberry decided to abandon the Mets for a $3 million-a-year deal with the Dodgers, some reporters responded by belittling his value to the New York team. "The

Mets won't miss Darryl Strawberry that much," one wrote, adding that "the Straw" was not likely to prove much of a bargain to the L.A. club either. Jose Canseco was roundly scolded for what writers saw as his lackluster play in the 1990 World Series. Anyone getting paid $5 million ought to put on a better show, that was the idea, and never mind the injuries that had plagued the Oakland star during the regular season.

Press comments regularly link criticisms of athletes to the amounts they make. "Why should they [tennis players] be paid handsomely as professional athletes and at the same time be coddled like babies?" Robert Kelleher wanted to know. McCallum: "Let's face it, my own exhaustive research suggests that 99% of the American public thinks that today's athletes are overpaid ingrates who aren't worth a portion of what they're making, and the other 1% thinks they're worse." It's not so much that professional athletes want higher pay and better working conditions or that they display such flaws as bad temper and arrogance that seems to be on people's minds. What really irks the critics is that athletes appear to think they can be as rich as they are and still make demands and display human foibles.

Or perhaps the irritation goes even deeper. We Americans love sports, and we love its stars . . . Babe Ruth . . . Red Grange . . . Jennifer Capriati . . . Michael Jordan. Supreme Court Justice Blackmun could spin off the names of eighty-eight in the game of baseball alone. Like Blackmun, like Oliver Wendell Holmes writing in *Federal League,* like Albert Spalding with his mythic Abner Doubleday, American sportswriters and fans imagine the sports legends of the past to have been highly principled superbeings, religiously devoted to their game and willing to sacrifice anything for it, far above such banalities as cash, comfort, pensions, and endorsements.

Perhaps some were. The NL's great turn-of-the-century shortstop Honus Wagner became so upset when he discovered that a tobacco company was distributing a card with his picture on it—this was before baseball cards came with bubble gum—that he demanded the company stop. Wagner neither smoked nor drank, and he didn't want to encourage others to either. That is why anyone looking at one of the rare Honus Wagner cards that did make it onto the market may be looking at upward of half a million dollars. Four hundred and ten thousand dollars was what NHLer Wayne Gretzky and a business partner paid for a Wagner in 1991.

But Wagner was an exception. Most sports figures of the past behaved as humanly as the rest of us—the public just didn't know about it. Babe Ruth was a drinker and a womanizer, and he made no effort to hide his failings when he traveled with reporters. The reporters' legendary reaction: "Gentlemen, I guess none of us saw that." Modern sportswriters don't just see it, they tell it; witness the one who tattled about Agassi's private conversation with his brother. If that present-day reporter had hung out with The Babe—or covered many other earlier athletic heroes—our picture of them might not be quite as idealized as it is. Or so the pros could defend themselves.

Professional athletes might also remind their critics that they aren't the only ones in American sport who occasionally combine human imperfection with the desire to prosper materially. U.S. Olympic Committee president Robert Helmick was forced to resign in 1991 in the wake of reports that he had accepted over a quarter of a million dollars in "consulting fees" from companies on the lookout for Olympic contracts. Also in 1991, USOC executive director Harvey Schiller was accused of having raised money grants to the U.S. ski team in return for free ski passes and equipment for himself.

Of course, the fact that some in sports management show signs of corruption doesn't excuse player "greed." But it may give us another perspective on that greed.

What is more, athletes could add, despite all their apparent wealth, power, and privilege, they are hardly at the top of the heap in the sports business. As Albert Spalding knew, there is a difference between capital and labor, and he and his friends took care to structure commercial sport's prototype so as to preserve that difference, with the former—leagues, associations, and their money—firmly in control of the latter—players. Even with free agency, megasalaries, and all the rest, Spalding's modern-day successors do a fair job of keeping it that way.

A number of factors conspire to help them out. In the first place, even without the rigid old reserve systems, clubs, leagues, and associations retain a large measure of power over players. That's partly because athletes recognize that if modern consumer sport is to profit, it must have strong central organization, capable of, for instance, squeezing the largest possible amounts of money out of broadcast executives. Consequently, most athletes willingly accept certain standards and limitations. As we saw, Japan's Ayako Okamoto submitted to banishment from a major golf tournament for the "crime" of not having initialed her entry form. Fiery Andre Agassi meekly paid the $25,000 fine imposed upon him by the ITA in the wake of the Grand Slam Cup affair. Monica Seles paid $6,000 after pulling out of Wimbledon competition at the last moment in 1991. In team sports, too, players may be kept in their place. Rookies are likely to have to work a set number of years under their original, perhaps none-too-generous, contracts before becoming free agents. And, of course, when a free agent signs even the richest new contract, it means agreeing to be bound for a new period of time. Just look at Rickey Henderson and the fabulous deal he thought he was getting in 1989.

In pro hockey, signing even the richest free-agent contract has its special hazards. A year after Scott Stevens joined the St. Louis Blues, for example, league arbitrators sent him to the New Jersey Devils. The reason: after signing Stevens, the Blues acquired Brendan Shanahan from the New Jersey club. Since the NHL still aims to limit its number of free agents, it penalizes teams that deal with them. For the Blues, the penalty was to make it up to the Devils for Shanahan's loss by giving the New Jersey team another star—Stevens. Stevens resisted the move, but discovered he had no choice. He and his family sold their house, packed up, and left St. Louis.

The second thing that helps keep management in its place and athletes in theirs is the fact that when organizational changes occur in sport—when rival leagues merge, for example—those doing the organizing cling to whatever monopolistic remnants they still enjoy. One such remnant: common new-player drafts. In the NFL and the NBA, the draft arrangement is that the team with the poorest won-lost record one year automatically gets first choice among that year's crop of eligible college players. The team with the best record gets last choice, and the teams in between fall into place accordingly. However, the system was fashioned to allow clubs a maximum of flexibility while limiting players to a minimum of the same commodity. If a team wanted to "sell" its picking-order rights to another in return for cash or an already established player, it might do so. Draftees, on the other hand, could negotiate only with whichever club owned the league-granted right to approach them. Only gradually has the system evolved to give draftees more freedom. As leagues expand and new leagues appear, players find more options open to them. In 1991, Notre Dame football star Raghib "Rocket"

Ismail spurned all NFL offers to sign with the Canadian Football League's Toronto franchise. Ismail's success in winning a $14 million four-year CFL contract will no doubt encourage other young players to continue challenging traditional sports monopolies.

Among the vestiges of the old monopolies that until recently remained to the detriment of players was the NFL's Plan B free agency scheme. Put into effect in 1989, Plan B permitted a club to decide at the end of each playing season which thirty-seven of its forty-seven team members it wanted to "protect," to keep for the next season. Protected players were strictly limited in their ability to negotiate new contracts with other teams. Unprotected players, on the other hand— Plan B free agents—were allowed to negotiate with whomever they wished. Plan B, says Peter King of *Sports Illustrated,* was "the NFL's way of proving to a federal court judge that free agency exist[ed] in the league." The "proof" was the demonstration by owners that they were allowing a measure of salary competition and thus not violating antitrust laws. However, a study conducted by the NFL itself showed that of 1,300-plus Plan B free agents in 1989 and 1990, only 124— under 10 percent—landed active playing jobs. Protected players, for their part, found themselves unable to compete freely for wages during their top playing years. This was hardly an arrangement that favored athletes, and in 1991, eight NFLers took the league to court over the issue. After a three-month trial, the court came down on the players' side, ruling that Plan B was illegal under federal antitrust law. At the same time, impressed by team owners' arguments that a total overturn of its reserve system threatened financial havoc for the league, the court left NFL officials free to work out other, less restrictive, limits on player freedom.

Third, when there is a dispute between a player and management, management may find relief outside the sports establishment. For example, a team owner may succeed in getting a court of law to force a player to fulfill what the owner sees as the player's contractual obligations. That's what the NBA's Boston Celtics did when Brian Shaw announced plans to ignore a contract that bound him to the Celts and play a second year on the Italian team with which he'd also signed. The court ruled in favor of Boston, saying that Shaw's Celts contract was the valid one. Shaw returned to Boston.

Also helping sports capitalists maintain the upper hand is their willingness to resort to hardball tactics upon occasion. The ITA's Grand Slam Cup plan to undermine the ATP attempt to win bigger tournament purses was one example of such tactics. A second was the preseason player lockout organized by baseball owners in 1990. The lockout, which kept team members from starting spring training and getting into shape for the season ahead, was designed to force players to accept limits on their arbitration rights. Sometimes, hardball methods turn sordid. When, in 1990, Yankees player Dave Winfield became involved in a contract dispute with owner George Steinbrenner, Steinbrenner went to the New York City criminal underworld for help. According to baseball commissioner Fay Vincent, who investigated the affair, Steinbrenner paid $40,000 to a shady character named Howard Spira in exchange for information he planned to use to discredit Winfield.

At other times, sports entrepreneurs carry their us-against-them way of doing business to miserly extremes. Cincinnati Reds pitcher José Rijo's 1991 contract called for him to get a $62,500 bonus if he threw 205 innings that season. Out five weeks with an ankle injury, Rijo nevertheless pitched 204 1/3 innings. He did *not* get the bonus. Equally mean-spirited, but far vaster in scope, was the attempt by the baseball owners of the mid-1980s to do players out of some of the salary negotiating rights they had won in the 1970s. Between 1985 and 1988, the owners secretly agreed to set limits on free agent salaries. Their collusion—prompted, says the *Wall Street Journal,* by then-commissioner Peter Ueberroth—denied up to 320 players the chance to compete fairly for wages. Arbitrators eventually intervened, ordering owners to repay players to the tune of $280 million. Players won that round—but what will owners, leagues, and associations think of next?

Professional athletes have no way of knowing, and that is one reason they give for holding out for all they can get when they can get it, even when their demands make them appear greedy or arrogant. Unless players keep on pressing, they say, they risk a return to the bad old days of artificially depressed wages and severely rationed benefits. Athletes believe they cannot afford to lose sight of the fact that despite the applause and the glory, they are sport's working class, its hired hands. They are the cogs—each with its own specialized function—in the complex machinery that is the team, the league, the association. While teams, leagues, and associations are institutions designed to endure over time, players come and go, interchangeable bits, necessary, but replaceable.

Take Jose Canseco. Marvelous player, but hardly the only six-foot, three-inch, 230-pound, athletically talented right-hander out there. High schools, colleges, the minor leagues, they're all full of hungry young players just itching for a change at the bigs. New free agents come along every year. Even though Oakland seemed willing to pay Canseco $23.5 million over the life of the contract he signed in 1990, that sum was only a fraction of what the team is worth: $225 million. Take Canseco out of the lineup for any reason and his team will go right on playing—and go right on being worth that same $225 million. Look at the so-what attitude with which New York said good-bye to Darryl Strawberry. One slugger was gone, but the Mets will be around for years.

Nor was it long before Canseco himself was also gone. Even as he headed out to take his turn at bat for Oakland in a game on the evening of August 31, 1992, the man whose fabulous contract had once stunned fans around the country was summoned back to the dugout and unceremoniously informed that he had just been traded to the Texas Rangers. Other millionnaire athletes drop out of the lineup or are forced off the field as a result of injuries. The very real risk of a career-ending injury is another reason athletes give for striking the best deals they can while they are young and healthy.

As we saw in chapter three, sports injuries are on the rise. And that in spite of all the protective gear available to modern athletes—elastic bandages, padding, helmets, masks, gloves, mouth guards, shin guards . . . up to thirty pounds' worth of protection for football players. According to Allen Guttmann, by the late 1980s the percentage of NFL players injured badly enough to miss one regular-season game was over 100. That means, he explains, "not that every NFL player is injured at least once each season, but that those who are not injured are more than offset by those who are injured several times." A bad elbow cost San Francisco quarterback Joe Montana the 1991–92 season, while a knee injury in the Philadelphia Eagles' first game put Randall Cunningham out of action for the remainder of the year. On November 17, 1991, Detroit Lions guard Mike Utley was paralyzed from the chest down when he fell and landed on his head. The next Sunday, four members of the New York Giants squad were knocked out of the game.

Hockey is another sport in which injury is rife. Writing in the *New York Times,* Joe Lapointe described what happened to twenty-three-year-old Brad Delgarno of the New York Islanders at the 1990 training camp: "Before his first scrimmage ended, Delgarno was lying on the ice, woozy, spitting blood, picking up two of his teeth—'like Chiclets,' he said—

from the ice. Four more teeth had been driven back from his lower jaw . . ." These were injuries suffered, not during a regular-season game, not in a do-or-die play-off series, but in the first practice of training camp.

Hockey and football players aren't the only ones risking injury. As pro tennis prepared for its 1991 Australian Open, John McEnroe announced his withdrawal from the tournament on account of a shoulder injury. Pete Sampras, citing shin splints, also bowed out. Defending champion Ivan Lendl faced play with painfully strained stomach muscles, while on the women's side (the women's *ward,* was how the *New York Times* expressed it), the event's 1990 runner-up, Mary Joe Fernandez, expected to be hampered by recent surgery on her hand. Knee surgery forced four-time U.S. champion and seven-time Wimbledon winner Martina Navratilova to join McEnroe and Sampras on the sidelines. All this in a noncontact sport!

For some athletes, injury means more than a missed contest or two. Mike Utley's paralysis is expected to be permanent. As 1991 began, dual-sport phenomenon Bo Jackson was earning $1 million a year as an outfielder for baseball's Kansas City Royals and $1.4 million a year more as a football running back for the Los Angeles Raiders. Then, on January 13, Jackson sustained a hip injury in a Raiders play-off game. The injury ended his football career and may have wiped out his baseball future—he came to bat just seventy-one times in 1991. Fortunately for him, Jackson was "greedy" enough to have negotiated a Raiders contract that gives him $4 million in disability insurance plus his salary. But no contract can give him back his chance to play.

Still, Jackson can count himself lucky. A hip is hardly the ultimate loss. "Since 1945," says Allen Guttmann, "more than 350 boxers have been killed in the ring or have died as an immediate consequence of injuries incurred there." Auto racing can be deadly, too. On November 30, 1990, race car driver Bill Vukovich, Jr., buried his twenty-eight-year-old son, Billy Vukovich 3d, killed while practicing for a race in Bakersfield, California. Thirty-five years earlier, Bill Jr. had lost his father when Bill Sr. crashed in attempting to win his third consecutive Indianapolis 500.

Why all the damage? Some is inevitable, given the strenuous nature of sports. But much is not. Guttmann finds artificial turf—so common in baseball and football stadiums—to blame for a good many injuries. He cites a 1974 study by Stanford University that "found that in 17 out of 17 categories, natural grass was safer to play on than . . . artificial surfaces." The NFL Players Association similarly contends that the slippery plastic is dangerous. So why don't teams stick to the real thing? Why don't coaches insist upon it? Why don't leagues make rules about it? Partly because artificial grass is cheaper to maintain and a necessity in indoor stadiums. Partly also because the name of a corporate sponsor can't be embedded in natural grass as it can in AstroTurf—to the substantial profit of the sports organizations that lease such space for advertising purposes. "In the calculations of franchise owners," Guttmann declares, "the economic benefits of artificial turf apparently outweigh the risks run by the players."

Another reason for sport's high rate of injury, some say, stems from the callousness with which some managers and coaches treat their injured players. And from the way some players treat themselves, too: "playing hurt" is a long-standing sports tradition. The injuries suffered by hockey's Brad Delgarno in training camp were inflicted on a Saturday. Delgarno was back on the ice the next Tuesday, the day *before* his four displaced lower teeth were removed.

Isn't it part of a coach's job—or the team doctor's—to protect players, even if it's from themselves? In theory, yes, but according to Guttmann and others, a more important part seems to be to patch up the injury, fill the athlete up with Novocain or some other chemical pain killer, and send him back out to play. This approach, says former NFL doctor Arnold J. Mandell, "breaks ribs, ruins knees, twists lives." Guttmann agrees, describing how the coach of the San Diego Sockers soccer team reacted when one player complained of a facial injury. The clubhouse doctor had diagnosed a fractured cheekbone, but the coach insisted it was no such thing. That particular doctor stuck to his guns and insisted upon treating the player, but others might not. Or might not be able to. The Cincinnati Reds team doctor, Michael Lawhon, resigned at the end of 1991 to protest what he saw as inadequate player care. Among his gripes: "a lack of support and honesty from the front office, continued second-guessing and misleading reports about injuries." On at least one major U.S. sports franchise, the team physician is also part owner of the club. What happens when an owner-doctor treats a player who's injured—and also a key to victory? Players and agents who suspect they know the answer may think they have good reason to demand contract clauses calling for medical evaluations by an independent expert.

Pros and their agents contend that there are good reasons for their other demands as well. Good reason for asking for signing bonuses, like the $3.5 million Canseco got the year before his 1990 contract went into effect. After all, teams, leagues, and associations get plenty of up-front cash. Advance and season ticket sales; rentals on luxury boxes equipped with television and private bars and bathrooms; income from broadcast deals; signage money; licensing fees for all sorts of logo-marked goods—it adds up to billions of dollars available as capital to be used or invested against future needs. Athletes remember the time—only a few years ago—when many of them ended their playing days financially broke, physically hurting, and untrained for any nonsports job. Why, they wonder, shouldn't they have as much right to financial protection as their bosses have? Guttmann points out that due to higher injury rates, the average length of an NFL career has dropped to 3.2 years, "not long enough to qualify a player for inclusion in the league's pension plan." If a player knows his chances of getting a pension at the end of his career are iffy, isn't it simply common sense for him to want a signing bonus at its outset? Players also remind their critics that as individuals, they do not qualify for the corporate tax breaks available to a Ted Turner or to Paramount Communications. Nor does the tax-paying public make the kind of capital investment in players that it does in franchises as, for example, when a city or county agrees to build a new stadium or arena to attract a new team or hang on to an old one.

There is good reason for players to demand improvements in pensions, medical care, and other benefits, too, they say. Workers in other industries get them. So do nonathletes working in sports. Umpires for major-league baseball walked off the job at the end of 1991 spring training over salary scales and other issues. Besides, if athletes have to go out and play on AstroTurf when they'd be safer on grass, why shouldn't some of the money saved—or earned—by installing the artificial stuff be devoted to nicer lounges or more considerate medical care? The men of the NFL have to let TV technicians call some of their time-outs so television—and the league and its teams—can profit from precisely timed advertising messages. So it is unreasonable for them to ask that some of that increased profit be diverted into better-equipped locker rooms or a pension fund? Football schedules keep baseball players from practicing before a championship game. If they complain, is that a sign of arrogance?

Professional athletes and their defenders also have something to say about the criticism aimed at their product-endorsement policies. To begin with, they maintain, while some make millions selling products, most make a good deal less— or nothing at all. "Endorsements are a pyramid," sports agent Leigh Steinberg told *TV Guide* in 1990, "and only a select few [players]—fewer than two dozen—do them in any significant way nationally." Even those two dozen may not retain their endorsement value for long. Some pros do commercials for a few seasons, then are passed over in favor of younger, fresher faces. Others may be barred from top contracts because advertisers feel uneasy about their off-the-field behavior. As of 1992, Jose Canseco's brushes with the law (traffic tickets and possession of an unregistered handgun) kept him from landing any major endorsements. Boxer Mike Tyson lost his $1 million-a-year Pepsi contract following a highly publicized divorce. After his 1992 conviction on a rape charge, his chances of representing any company ever again appeared to be zero. Some players—quarterback Dan Marino of the Miami Dolphins is one—can't get big endorsement deals because their ho-hum teams languish in the lower half of the standings. Injuries can hurt, too. After Bo Jackson damaged his hip, no one was sure what would become of his $2 million "Bo Knows" Nike endorsement campaign. "Does Bo, Hurt, Know as Much?" asked a headline in the *New York Times* business section. "It certainly does not make sense for sporting goods companies to use an injured sports celebrity" was one advertising consultant's answer. According to another, even if Jackson made a baseball comeback while failing to play football again, he might not regain his commercial value. "With a lot of the glitter gone, his fees would certainly be reduced." Magic Johnson saw his endorsement ads fading from the screen after he announced that he had the virus that causes AIDS. Like an athletic career itself, product endorsement can be an uncertain business.

For the companies buying the endorsements though, they are pretty much of a sure thing. Michael Jordan has done well out of his deal with Nike, but Nike has done far, far better. Each pair of Air Jordans the company sells at $130 costs $30 to produce and another $38.75 to promote and market. That leaves $61.25 in profit. Nike posted $2.2 billion in sales in 1990 with net profits of $243 million. Between January and August of that year, the company's stock jumped 72 percent in value. And it was Nike, not Jordan, that dreamed up the ad campaign that has kids committing murder. Nike, not Jordan, invented the notion that acquiring $130 shoes is as easy as "Just do it."

It's not just the companies offering endorsement contracts that benefit along with athletes from sport's ties to commerce, players could add. Teams, leagues, and associations are as eager as any athlete to work out endorsement/sponsorship arrangements. Take in a basketball game, and what do you see? At the Seattle Coliseum, ten separate bulletin boards advertising Alaska Airlines, Blockbuster Video, and other companies; brightly lit Coca-Cola signs over the entrance-ways, visitors' side folding chairs that bear the Coke logo, computer-generated ads—sixty-five during the course of a single match—chasing each other across the scoreboard.

Corporate "blood money"—as Health and Human Services Secretary Louis Sullivan described sponsorship dollars from cigarette and beer companies—makes its way into team, league, and association pockets. Tennis lends its support—weightier than that of any single player or group of players—to the Virginia Slims tournament. "The players feel very comfortable with Virginia Slims," says Anne Person, managing director of the Women's International Pro Tennis Council.

Apparently the council does anyway. NASCAR relies upon brewery sponsorship to finance its events and had no patience with Sullivan's requests for the group to end its relationship with the beer companies. "As long as [alcohol] is a legal product . . . we'll keep doing it [taking its money]," one auto speedway owner said in 1991. Professional golf gets $16 million a year from Johnnie Walker whiskey. *Newsweek* magazine reports that blood money is trickling down through pro sports—Anheuser-Busch sponsors women's beach volleyball, while Miller beer takes care of the men—to what were once mere children's games. In 1988, Southern Comfort, the whiskey maker, established the Southern Comfort Finger Flick Tournament, sponsoring contests in bars nationwide. All across America, if *Newsweek* is to be believed, tens of thousands of contestants busy themselves snapping bits of folded paper to score "goals" and make points. And—tiddlywinks again—in England, the game gets backing from Heineken beer money, which pays for televising events. Tiddlywinks may yet make it to U.S. screens. As the 1990s began, the North American Tiddlywinks Association was considering a TV sponsorship deal.

Even when it comes to a tragedy like murder, individual athletes are not the only ones associated with the crime. More teenagers have been robbed or killed for jackets and other pieces of clothing bearing team logos than for their celebrity-endorsed shoes. Somehow, though, crimes committed for the sake of team paraphernalia don't rate the headlines that sneaker-murders do. Michael Jordan is a big star and a high-visibility personality. He is a man who makes daily appearances on television screens around the country, a sports hero with whom millions identify. Any murder involving his name is bound to get greater press attention than one centered on a more diffuse entity such as a team. As for the business partners or corporation that owns the team, they receive hardly any public attention at all. Nor does the corporation that produces the longed-for clothing, the ad agency that promotes it, or the store that stocks it. Yet each is an essential link in the chain that can end in a killing.

It's their high visibility, professional athletes might argue, that attracts criticism all along the line. Being in the spotlight, they get an unfair share of the blame for doing in sports what an awful lot of other people are also doing in sports and other industries: making a fortune.

There is something to that argument, *New York Times* reporter Ira Berkow concedes, pointing out that nobody seems to worry about show-business people or billionaire businessmen receiving outrageously high recompense for their contributions to society. By some estimates, the chairman of the Coca-Cola company, Roberto C. Goizueta, took home $86 million in 1991 alone. Carlyle C. Douglas of the *New York Times* tells us that Jack Nicholson earned $10 million for his portrayal of The Joker in the 1989 movie *Batman*. Bill Cosby earns about $100 million a year as a comic, actor, author (assisted by a ghost writer), and endorser of products. Singer Michael Jackson got an $18 million advance on a new album in 1990. So what? "They make, and we nod; it's the American way," Douglas wrote. Why should it be any different for professional athletes? Surely they are as entitled as anyone else to demand good working conditions and high salaries. After all, Berkow points out, "The money is there." It's money that at least one of Berkow's *Times* colleagues would prefer to have going to players than to their bosses. "I'd rather see Don Mattingly have the money than George Steinbrenner," says George Vecsey. "The ball players, after all, can throw and run and hit a curve ball . . . The owners, on the other hand, merely own."

Chapter 5

Problems, Problems, Problems

All businesses have problems, and the sports business is no exception. Problems of supply and demand, problems linked to profits and losses, problems related to salaries, sales, taxes, and so on—commercial sport knows them all. In addition, sport faces some special, perhaps unresolvable, problems of its own.

One headline-making sports problem is drugs. The drugs may be legal—alcohol, for example—or illegal, marijuana, cocaine, or heroin. They may be, like alcohol, marijuana, cocaine, and heroin, of the so-called recreational variety. Or they may be what are known as "vocational" drugs, substances like the amphetamines ("speed") or muscle-building anabolic steroids that some players rely upon to enhance their athletic output. But whatever they are, and however they may be used, drugs permeate modern sport.

To begin with, there is alcohol. Scarcely had the 1991 baseball season gotten underway when two members of the Philadelphia Phillies squad, center fielder Len Dykstra and catcher Darren Daulton, were seriously injured in an early-morning car crash. A blood alcohol test showed Dykstra at well over the legal limit for driving. A month earlier, retired horse racing legend Willie Shoemaker was paralyzed while driving drunk, and a month before that Boston Celtics guard Charles

Smith faced charges of driving under the influence and motor vehicle homicide in the deaths of two Boston University students. On Christmas Day 1989, former New York Yankee player and manager Billy Martin was killed in an automobile accident. Both Martin and a friend who was with him in the car were legally intoxicated. The NHL's Mike Keenan, coach of the Chicago Blackhawks, was picked up for drunk driving in 1990. Alcohol is equally in evidence on the college and secondary school level. In 1990, University of Maryland basketball coach Gary Williams was fined for drunk driving while Cleveland State coach Kevin Mackey was ordered by an Ohio judge into a drug and alcohol rehabilitation center. That same year, sixteen of the top athletes at one Long Island high school were caught drinking. Such alcohol-related sports stories represent just a few of those that make headlines almost daily.

Then there are illegal drugs. Early in the NBA's 1991–92 season, Dallas Mavericks center Roy Tarpley was banned from league play after refusing to take a drug test. Tarpley had flunked two previous tests. Yankee pitcher Steve Howe was arrested in December 1991 on a cocaine possession charge, his sixth cocaine-related offense. In 1990, jockey Patrick Valenzuela, a Kentucky Derby winner the year before, was suspended indefinitely from racing after testing positive for drugs. At the same time, Grant Fuhr, goaltender for hockey's Edmonton Oilers, owned up to a history of cocaine abuse. Boxer Sugar Ray Leonard confessed in 1991 to an earlier cocaine habit, and so did Olympic speed skater Mary Docter. For college players, too, illegal drugs pose a threat. University of Maryland basketball star Len Bias was riding high as the number-one draft pick of the World Champion Boston Celtics in the spring of 1986. After a day of contract talks with the Celts, Bias felt like celebrating. He did—with cocaine—

overdosed, and died. Three members of a Maine high school hockey team were suspended after buying marijuana in 1992. Again, stories like these are only a few of many.

Apart from recreational drugs are vocational ones. Allen Guttmann says that the first athlete believed to have attempted to improve his showing chemically was Welsh bicyclist Arthur Linton, who swallowed the stimulant strychnine in advance of an 1886 race. Strychnine—deadly in all but the most minuscule of amounts—is not a safe substance to fool around with, but Linton was lucky. Other, less daring, athletes of his day turned to substances like caffeine for a competitive edge. Then, in the 1930s, amphetamines appeared on the market.

Medically, amphetamines may be used as nasal inhalers, to suppress the appetites of dieters, or to treat depression. They are also capable, in the short run, of increasing stamina and prolonging endurance, making them attractive to athletes determined to force themselves to and beyond the point of physical exhaustion. But amphetamines have dangerous side effects, particularly on the heart. In 1960, a Danish cyclist collapsed after taking amphetamines during an Olympic race, the first modern Olympian to die in competition. But it was not until another cyclist died from amphetamines seven years later that the IOC acted, setting up a commission to study ways of dealing with the problem. By then, as many as 25 percent of athletes worldwide may have been using performance enhancers. By then also, those enhancers included anabolic steroids.

Steroids affect the body through its hormonal system. First available commercially in the late 1950s, their ability to help build muscle mass and strength quickly won them favor among athletes, especially among body builders, swimmers, and track and field competitors. "The curse of those sports that require great strength," Guttmann calls steroids.

A curse because athletes who turn to steroids, like those who depend upon amphetamines, must be prepared to suffer the consequences: increased risk of heart and liver disease, sterility in men, and, in women, the appearance of masculine characteristics, such as facial hair growth. Lyle Alzado, fifteen-year veteran of the NFL and a steroid user for over two decades, blamed the tumor found in his brain in 1991 on the drugs. Alzado's doctor agrees that steroids, which depress the body's immune system, may have been linked to his particular type of cancer.

Steroids are also a curse since despite their side effects, their muscle-building capabilities make them irresistible to thousands of athletes, especially to young ones whose musculature is not yet fully developed. Although the nonmedical use of steroids is illegal, and though the IOC banned them in 1975, eight athletes at the next year's Games were discovered to have taken them. All eight were disqualified, yet their expulsion did little to discourage others from following in their footsteps. By the 1980s, an Olympic contender from Finland was charging that "at least 80 percent of top sportsmen are slaves of hormone products."

One "slave" was Canadian sprinter Ben Johnson, who began using steroids in 1981. Seven years later at the Summer Olympics in Seoul, South Korea, a hugely muscled Johnson won the gold medal in the 100-meter dash, setting a new world's record in the process. But a post-race drug test revealed that he had taken enough steroids to have improved his performance level by as much as 4 percent. Johnson was stripped of his medal and record—and of his other records as well—and permanently banned from official competition.

The punishment sounded severe. And so it should have been. For Johnson's offense was no simple infraction of the rules—forgetting to initial an entry form or failing to compete as planned. Nor did he merely fall victim to a drug habit, such as alcoholism, as can happen to anyone in any field of endeavor. What Johnson did was to undermine the very spirit of modern sport. Secretly resorting to a substance that gave him a hidden advantage over his competition, Johnson violated a fundamental sports principle, that of fair play.

As it turned out, however, Johnson's punishment was not so severe, after all. We'll see more about that in just a minute. But meantime, let's take a look at why so many athletes continue to use steroids. The drugs are illegal, and taking them can result in suspension or worse. Their physical dangers are manifest. Yet a U.S. government study released in 1990 showed that a quarter million American adolescents, mostly boys, use steroids, and indicated that the number is growing. Along with that report came news that five American track and field stars, two of them U.S. record holders and Olympic silver medalists, had been suspended from competition after testing positively for steroids. Why do they do it?

For many athletes, the reason is simple: steroids produce winners—and not just on the field. If Ben Johnson's steroid use had gone undetected in Seoul, he would have come home with an Olympic gold medal. He probably would have had some rich product-endorsement contracts to boot. Big muscles, athletes know, can translate into big bucks.

But a more important reason that steroids and other vocational drugs persist in sport goes beyond athletes themselves. All too often, it seems, the very people—coaches, managers, owners, and the like—who should be doing the most to get such substances out of sport permit, even encourage, their use. Sportswriter Leonard Koppett notes that it was bosses, not players, who introduced vocational drugs into sport to begin with. "The performance-enhancing drugs, from Novocain through anabolic steroids, were invariably prescribed *originally* by well-meaning doctors and trainers," Koppett wrote. Of course they were. In sports like football and hockey, where team members are expected to play hurt, powerful painkillers like Novocain are a must. Without them, how could players keep on going? And if players can't keep going, what happens to the game? To ticket sales and advertising revenues? The answers are obvious, and one reason, says former football pro David Meggyesy, is that "most NFL trainers do more dealing in these drugs than the average junky."

Meggyesy could be exaggerating, but his point is worth considering. Also worth considering is the suggestion that sports officials need to take more responsibility for educating players about the dangers of drugs of all types, not just performance enhancers. Why? Because athletes may be more vulnerable than a lot of other people to their addictive lure. Guttmann suggests that athletes see their success and wealth as charms to protect them from harm, even from the harm of drugs. "Talented athletes are accustomed to special treatment," he says. "Teenaged millionaire athletes are among the most fawned upon media celebrities." It doesn't take long, Guttmann goes on, for young sports stars to convince themselves that they're different from regular people. "Ordinary mortals might become addicts, the lionized athlete tells himself. *He* will have the universal safe conduct of his fame." So he, or she, falls victim to a habit that sports authorities could be doing more to prevent. Guttmann also reminds us that many athletes grow up in inner-city neighborhoods where illegal drugs are "commonplace" and using them is nothing out of the ordinary.

As for the legal drug alcohol, it, too, needs to be taken more seriously by sports management. Writing about Lenny Dykstra's drunk-driving accident, *New York Times* baseball reporter Claire Smith reminded readers that until recently, "drinking in the clubhouse . . . was not only tacitly approved but funded by teams." Philadelphia Phillies owner Bill Giles remembered when his team supplied after-game beer for players. "Players used to stick four or five cans in their pockets on the way out," he recalled. Phillies management no longer offers free drinks, and other clubs have either banned beer in the locker room or set limits on its consumption. Nevertheless, alcohol continues to be a mainstay in the sports world.

"Beer and professional sports go together in this country," says Christine Lubinski, public policy director for the National Council on Alcoholism and Drug Dependence, the nation's leading nongovernment drug-awareness agency. Lubinski points to Budweiser beer's "Bud Player of the Week" award as an example of how teams and leagues promote alcoholic consumption. One New York high school quarterback, suspended from his team for drinking, regards alcohol as an inescapable part of sport. "When you watch a football game, what's the commercial you see?" he asks. "Bud. Miller. It's like hand in hand: football and beer." Baseball, too. "Baseball is built on beer money," says former Yankee Roger Maris, who became a distributor for the product after leaving the game. Other sports are similarly tied to beer and other forms of alcohol. Just look at the signage and listen to the names of sponsors and advertisers.

Still another reason for sport's failure to put an end to its drug problem may lie in the very programs that are supposed to detect drug use. Testing is by no means universal in sport, and where it does exist, it is not always adequate. One reason for that is its cost. "In 1986," says Murray Sperber, a sportswriter now teaching at Indiana University, "the NCAA began testing athletes for eighty-one substances . . . at its championship events." The program cost about $300 per individual tested, or $950,000 a year. Within two years, the price of a single state-of-the-art test had jumped to $1,000. At that price, complete tests are too expensive to conduct on a whole-sale basis. The NCAA administered 14,000 drug tests in 1990—up from 5,000 four years before—but only in its Division I football were tests carried out twelve months of the year.

Similar cost factors and consequent lack of thorough test-ing are problems for other associations and leagues. The lack of thoroughness leaves drug-taking athletes knowing that if they simply abstain for a few days or weeks before a sched-uled test, they will probably pass it. Other ways athletes cheat on the tests include submitting false urine samples, using masking chemicals to conceal the presence of steroids, or switching from synthetic steroids to the hormones that direct human growth. As of the early 1990s, human growth hor-mones were virtually impossible to identify in tests.

Another problem for drug-testing programs has been resis-tance from athletes. Some NFL team owners began calling for testing in the 1980s, but the Players' Association objected, arguing that tests would violate its members' right to privacy. College athletes have objected, too, on the grounds that test-ing implies a presumption of guilt and that, as U.S. citizens, they must be assumed innocent of wrongdoing unless there is evidence to the contrary. A more technical objection comes from Pat Connolly, professional track coach and three-time Olympian. Contrary to official claims, Connolly says, even state-of-the-art tests cannot catch all drug users. We know that Ben Johnson's steroid use was uncovered at the 1988 Olympics. But, Connolly charges, a female competitor can take enough steroids to enhance her performance by 7 per-cent—almost twice the increase Johnson achieved—and not be caught. Women, it seems, can increase their strength sig-nificantly from amounts of hormone so small as to go undetected, while men must take much more to achieve the same degree of gain. "Until data has been gathered and studied from comprehensive . . . testing of male and female athletes for two generations," Connolly says, testing programs will be little more than gimmicks that mistreat athletes by rewarding and punishing them arbitrarily.

Punishing them arbitrarily while enabling sports entrepreneurs to hang on to their paying audiences, critics add. As they see it, drug-testing programs are so spotty, inexact, and easy to cheat on that they are worthless as a means of eliminating sport's drug problem. In fact, the critics add, the tests aren't even aimed at eliminating it. Testing's true goal—like the goal of sports drug policies overall—is a public relations one: convincing ticket-buying and television-viewing fans that sport's drug problem is under control.

Are sports drug policies shaped more by a concern for appearances than by genuine interest in the health and well-being of the players? In some cases, they seem to be. While NFL owners were pointing the finger at the Players Association for speaking out against testing in the eighties, they themselves were calling some tests "an invasion of privacy." This according to Dr. Arnold Mandell, whom we met in chapter four. Mandell adds that when he offered to conduct a drug clinic for NFL team doctors, Commissioner Pete Rozelle nixed the idea as "bad public relations." Asked whether any of the coaches he worked for on three different NFL teams were aware that he was on steroids, Lyle Alzado said that they had to have been, but that they "just coached and looked the other way."

Will football go on looking the other way? The signs are mixed. A new drug policy instituted by the NFL in 1991 included a four-day suspension for players convicted of drunk driving. First to be nailed under the revised policy was Kevin

Butler of the Chicago Bears. He got a fine, no suspension. The day Butler got his good news, two players for the Indianapolis Colts were arrested for drunkenly threatening customers with a pistol at a fast-food restaurant. Hauled off by police at 1:00 A.M., the two were released on bail and back on the practice field that afternoon.

Other sports officials have displayed a similar slap-on-the-wrist approach to drug abuse. Atlanta Braves pitcher Otis Nixon, suspended for taking cocaine while his team was chasing the National League pennant in 1991, was welcomed back to the club before the year was out. Welcomed back with a contract good for as much as $8.1 million by the end of the '94 season. Steve Howe's 1991 cocaine-possession arrest led Commissioner Fay Vincent to hit him with a permanent suspension. Yankee management, thoroughly upset at losing a player of Howe's stature, appealed the ruling. It was eventually overturned by an arbitrator. Jockey Pat Valenzuela, another asset to his profession, saw his "indefinite" 1990 suspension lifted in 1991. As for the National Basketball Association, league spokesman Brian McIntyre said in 1991 that although drugs and alcohol are discussed at rookie seminars, the league has no ongoing program to address the subject. "We don't view it as an NBA players' problem," he told the *New York Times*. John Ziegler, president of the National Hockey League from 1977 until 1992, never saw it as a problem for that organization either. But it has been: witness Grant Fuhr. And how did Ziegler deal with Fuhr? First, by suspending him from play for a year. Second, by lifting that suspension after just five months. And Ben Johnson? How did he fare in the wake of his suspension?

Not badly. In 1990, the IOC revoked that portion of its punishment—and Johnson got right to work practicing for the 1992 Games. A "permanent" suspension that ends after only two years without forcing an erring athlete to miss even a single set of Olympics? Why shouldn't Johnson—and other athletes—take antidrug rhetoric with a grain of salt?

Drugs are not the only problem facing sport today. Another is gambling.

Games and gambling have long been associated, and, in fact, "gaming" is another word for gambling. Bets on athletic contests were common in ancient Egypt and Rome and among native North and South Americans. During the Middle Ages, Europeans might wager on tournament play or on the outcomes of individual combat. Richard Mandell, however, points out that the kind of betting done in ancient and medieval times was not like betting today. That is because back then, victory was believed to be determined, not by natural ability, but by God—or the gods. Wagers were therefore more a matter of faith than of reasoning based on objective estimates of an athlete's abilities.

Reasoned, or rational, betting, like so much of sport itself, developed largely in England. Up until the seventeenth century, that betting tended to be freakish in nature—wagers placed on races between scantily dressed girls, pregnant women, runners pushing wheelbarrows, and the like. Over time, though, betting took on a more modern appearance. Six thousand pounds is said to have been laid out on a straightforward footrace in 1618. By the 1700s, the English were further rationalizing betting with elementary handicapping techniques and by matching human contestants according to size and age and seeing to it that competing horses carried similar weights. England's New World settlers brought rational betting to this country.

But while betting in both England and America was popular and a built-in part of sports like horse racing and such games as poker and dice, it was frowned upon by some, especially by those of a religious turn of mind. "How would it look," the editor of a Georgia church publication scolded in 1840, "for Baptists or Methodists to be seen playing cards and running horses?" Traces of such attitudes linger today. Horse and dog racing remain illegal in some states. And until 1989, wagering on such sports events as football and basketball games was against the law everywhere but Nevada.

Against the law, but an everyday activity nonetheless. Surveys show that by the end of the 1980s, one-third or more of Americans were betting regularly at the races or on team contests. Conservative estimates set sports gambling at about $58 billion a year. The estimates suggested that close to two-thirds of that amount was being bet illegally. Other estimates placed the illegal betting figure at closer to $80 billion.

How do sports authorities feel about gambling, legal and otherwise? In part, their attitude reflects the one that helped shape baseball's reaction to the Black Sox scandal of 1919. Sports entrepreneurs know that gambling invites cheating and threatens to undermine sport by depriving it of its genuine competitiveness. Teams and leagues, horrified at the thought of losing that money-attracting element, are adamant about dissociating themselves and everyone else in their sport from the least public hint of gambling involvement.

The disassociations can be dramatic. As we saw in chapter four, New York Yankees owner George Steinbrenner was investigated by baseball commissioner Fay Vincent after it was rumored that he had paid Howard Spira $40,000 for damaging information about outfielder Dave Winfield. Vincent's investigation ended in his ordering Steinbrenner to remove himself from day-to-day Yankee club operations. The punishment, however, had nothing to do with Steinbrenner's offense against Winfield. It was inspired by the fact that Spira was known to have connections to gambling operations.

More dramatic than the discipline meted out to Steinbrenner was that reserved for Cincinnati Reds manager Pete Rose in 1989 by then-commissioner A. Bartlett Giamatti. Rose was—is—one of baseball's all-time standouts, an eighteen-year playing veteran of the Reds and holder of the record for most-ever career base hits, 4,256. But Rose was also a compulsive gambler, and Giamatti had evidence that he had bet on baseball games, including the games of the team he was managing. That was enough for the commissioner. After all, how could fans be sure manager Rose wasn't ordering playing strategy based on gambler Rose's wagers? How could they be positive Rose wouldn't manipulate the lineup or the pitching rotation for his own private gain? Giamatti ordered Rose placed on the permanently ineligible list, banned from baseball for life. Two years later, the directors of baseball's Hall of Fame adopted a new rule deliberately designed to render Rose permanently ineligible for membership in that institution.

Gambling taints other sports. In college basketball, it has created what Allen Guttmann calls the "permanent crisis." Basketball betting is based, not on wins and losses, but upon the point spread, the difference between the contending teams' final scores. So fixes, too, are organized around the point spread. Bettors analyze each team, calculating in such factors as season records and particular strengths and weaknesses, and wager on one to win by a certain number of points over the other. All the fixer has to do to make sure of walking off with the bettors' money is to reduce that number of points. And reducing it is as simple as paying one or more players on the favored team to "shave points" by deliberately missing a few floor shots or free throws. Gambling fixes have occurred in college basketball since the 1920s, with major scandals erupting in 1951, 1961, and 1985. The 1985 affair involved five Tulane University players and three outside fixers and ended with the elimination of Tulane's basketball program.

Despite the discipline, gambling persists—perhaps because the discipline is not always final or consistent. Tulane did lose its basketball program, but only temporarily, and John Williams, one of the players charged in the scandal, went on to win a $675,000 contract from the NBA's Cleveland Cavaliers. In 1990, Williams re-signed with the Cavs for $5 million a year. Jim Valvano, fired from his coaching job with North Carolina State's basketball team in 1990 after point-shaving charges were made against him, was promptly hired as a broadcast analyst by ABC-TV. Although disciplined by baseball, the USOC kept George Steinbrenner on as vice president.

Even baseball, with its searing memories of the 1919 World Series, displays a surprising indifference toward gambling allegations as long as those allegations do not attract undue attention. Rose and Steinbrenner were not the only men in the game linked to gambling in 1989 and 1990. Craig Neff and Jill Lieber of *Sports Illustrated* name others—Dave Winfield himself, for one. Also Lou Piniella, who replaced Rose as manager of the Reds, and retired catcher Bob Boone, then in the front office of the Kansas City Royals. The commissioner's office declined to investigate any of the three. "Bad Job, Baseball," Lieber and Neff scolded in an *SI* headline. Equally questionable in the eyes of some fans was the commissioner's decision to allow George Steinbrenner back into the game in time for the 1993 season.

Why sport's failure to confront its gambling problem and deal with it once and for all? The answer seems to come down to a matter of mixed feelings. Sports gambling may be anathema to administrators eager to sell the idea of competitive integrity, but it is also extremely popular. Team owners and league and association officials know that millions of fans are attracted to sport—buying tickets and following it on television—precisely because it does afford such exciting betting opportunities. So the officials' dilemma becomes one of enabling those fans to do, in good faith, something that is against the law in most of the country while distancing themselves and everyone else in the sport from any hint of that something. Or as James Heffernan, NFL public relations director, explains, "It's the perception that teams and players are involved [in gambling] that we object to." What about the reality?

The question is urgent. U.S. sports betting—legal sports betting—is on the upsurge. Where horse and dog racing are permitted, on-track betting is already a state-licensed business. In a few states, Offtrack Betting—OTB—is permitted. New York adopted OTB in 1971, taxing it as a means of pulling extra money into state coffers. Connecticut and Nevada have followed suit. Betting on team sports, legal only in Nevada prior to 1989, was introduced in Oregon that year as part of the state's official lottery system. (Oregon, like thirty-four other states, the District of Columbia, Puerto Rico, and the U.S. Virgin Islands, runs a lottery as a means of raising money to help fund public projects.) Since September 1989, Oregon football fans have been able to use the lottery to wager on the outcomes of anywhere from four to fourteen NFL games. Sports betting has also been made legal in Delaware, Montana, and North Dakota.

Other states might like to copy their example. Thousands of lawmakers and public officials nationwide already regard lotteries as a terrific alternative to new or higher taxes. Allowing those lotteries to cash in on the enthusiasm for sports gambling will mean even greater revenue for the states, they believe. Besides, the argument goes, if Americans are going to bet on sports anyway—at the rate of at least $58 billion a year—why not encourage them to do so legally? Thirty-seven nations outside the United States operate and tax sports gambling programs, advocates of legalized sports betting add. Why shouldn't we?

Because gambling is a bad business all round, betting opponents answer. About 5 percent of those who begin gambling go on to develop the kind of compulsive habit that destroyed Pete Rose's career. States shouldn't be encouraging others to follow his lead. They especially shouldn't be promoting gambling when it involves sport, so popular among young people. How are kids—eager to look like their favorite athletes, to dress like them, to *be* like them—going to react when they perceive them as part of a gambling operation? As for the notion that legalized sports betting will take bettors away from illegal bookmakers, antigambling activists say that's nonsense. The illegal game will always be more attractive to gamblers than any game a state can provide. For one thing, illegal bookies offer better odds and bigger payoffs than states do. For another, illegal operators, unlike states, provide credit to luckless gamblers. That's quite an inducement, given how many gamblers end up broke. In 1991, critics of state-sponsored sports gambling announced their support for a proposed federal law to prohibit such activity in the states where it was not yet legal. Chief sponsor of the bill was New Jersey senator Bill Bradley, a former basketball star for Princeton and the New York Knicks.

The sports establishment, including major-league baseball, the NFL, the NBA, the National Collegiate Athletic Association, and the U.S. Olympic Committee, was quick to endorse Bradley's proposal. But how sincere were such groups really? At the very moment it was urging federal action against legalized sports betting, the USOC was putting the finishing touches on a betting scheme of its own. Timed to coincide with the 1992 Olympics, the USOC's program called for it to sell blocks of lottery tickets to states, which would then offer those tickets to the public through their regular lottery outlets. By mid-1991, fifteen states had agreed to the deal. The USOC was hoping to raise $2 million before the 1992 Games and $25 million by 1996, money that would go toward the $300 million it currently costs to house and train U.S. athletes over each four-year Olympic cycle. Apparently the USOC distinguishes between gambling *on* sports and gambling *for* sports.

So, perhaps, would other sports organizations. Jim Wimsatt, director of New Hampshire's state lottery, maintains that the NFL, NBA, and such groups would drop their objections to state-sponsored sports gambling in a hurry if the states offered to split the profits with them. "As soon as any state sports gambling operation volunteers to share revenues with the leagues," says Wimsatt, "it will not only be accepted, it will be blessed. They [the leagues] simply want a slice of the pie." Sport's mixed messages on gambling—punishments for some, no action whatsoever on others, tolerance for recurrent college basketball scandals—suggest he may have a point.

A third major problem dogging sport today is that of discrimination. It comes in two forms: racism and sexism.

Sexism has a long history in sports and games. That's not surprising, considering the physical differences between men and women, as well as the fact that many societies have cast men as strong and aggressive and women as frail and needing protection. From primitive times, women's games, where they existed at all, must have been conducted separately from men's. At the ancient Olympics, women were not even permitted in the stands. They were, however, among the avid spectators at

Rome's ghastly gladiatorial contests. The high-born ladies of medieval Europe were onlookers, too, serving what sports historian Peter McIntosh calls their "supreme social function" of presiding at tournaments, graciously applauding the accomplishments of their menfolk. Peasant women, less willing to be relegated to the cheerleading role, plunged right into village games. In nineteenth-century America, public attacks on the new freedom that was beginning to allow girls and women to play croquet or ride bicycles were not uncommon. Such activities, declared one righteous gentleman, were "innovations for starting nice girls . . . down the skids to perdition."

Over time, the criticism lessened. Women's tennis was introduced in the 1870s, and the first women to enter the Olympics did so in 1900. Golfer Margaret Abbot became the first American woman to win an Olympic gold medal that year. Yet in 1920, the IOC was still refusing to allow women to compete at so rough a sport as field hockey, and in 1942 U.S. sports groups rejected the 100-yard dash as too vigorous an event for females. The first regular intercollegiate women's sports teams were organized in 1963, but it was to be another four years before women won the opportunity to compete in national varsity championships. Today, women are still limited as to the sports they can play for big money. Ice skating, tennis, and golf, yes. But even top female players in a game like basketball have little future beyond college. At least they have little future in the United States, although they can try out for a spot on a European or Australian team. But in general, as their male counterparts aim for the pros, female players prepare to retire.

That's retire, not go into coaching or managing. Women are not hired to help run the men's teams that dominate professional sport. Even at the college level, sport is so male-oriented that in 1988 only 48 percent of the coaches on women's college teams were other women. Just 16 percent of the Athletic Directors (ADs) of women's sports programs were women. The imbalance seems all the more striking given that in the mid-1970s, 95 percent of women's sports ADs were female, while 92 percent of women's teams had women coaches.

What happened? Once again, money is involved. In 1972, Congress passed a measure intended to put women's sports programs on a par with men's. The new law required high schools and colleges that received federal funds to provide equal athletic opportunities for both sexes. At first, the law worked. Women's sports programs were established at some schools and expanded at others, and an Association of Intercollegiate Athletics for Women (AIAW) was organized.

Unfortunately for both the programs and the AIAW, the National Collegiate Athletic Association saw the women's group as a threat to its monopolistic control of the country's college sports industry. The NCAA—largely male and composed at the top of a tightly knit group of former university ADs—had no intention of losing that control. It attacked the AIAW directly, offering women's sports programs NCAA memberships at rates below those of the AIAW. The NCAA also rearranged its championship play-offs, scheduling its women's events to conflict with the AIAW's. By 1982, the women's group had collapsed. "Another notch on the cartel's gun," Murray Sperber calls the NCAA coup, one that "gave new meaning to the term *predatory*."

Along with devastating the AIAW, the NCAA gutted the equal-funding provisions of Congress's 1972 law. In 1984, lawyers acting for the group obtained a Supreme Court ruling that allowed schools to narrow their interpretations of those provisions. As a result, says Sperber, "In 1987, at the main campus of the University of Arkansas, the athletic department spent one dollar in ten on women's sports." Sperber quotes the Arkansas AD as saying that this ratio "is similar to differences at most major colleges." In the future, that unfair ratio may change. During its 1991–92 term, the Supreme Court issued a decision allowing for monetary penalties against schools that refuse to comply with Congress's 1972 measure.

Yet after college, most women athletes remain stranded on the wrong side of a money gap. *Forbes* magazine's 1990 catalogue of the thirty top sports money-makers included twenty-eight men and only two women, tennis pros Steffi Graf and Gabriela Sabatini. Twenty years ago, not even those two would have made the list. Prizes in men's tennis tournaments were routinely set at many times those offered to women. The disparity between the purses at the 1970 Pacific Southwest Championships—$12,500 for the men versus $1,500 for the women—provoked tennis star Billie Jean King and others into mounting a boycott aimed at compelling tennis officials to increase cash rewards for female players. When the officials balked at the idea, King and her fellow boycotters went on to establish the rich Virginia Slims circuit. Perhaps it is partly their awareness of what the Slims tour meant to women's tennis twenty years ago that makes today's players hesitate to protest its links to tobacco.

There is another aspect to sexism in sports that cannot be ignored. Too often, male athletes display attitudes toward women that go beyond the merely patronizing to the violent and abusive. Mike Tyson, the world's youngest heavyweight boxing champion ever at age nineteen in 1986, was sentenced to prison six years later after being found guilty of rape. On college campuses, Gerald Eskenazi reports in the *New York Times*, "athletes are involved in a disproportionate number of rapes and other sexual assaults." His assertion is corroborated by the Philadelphia *News*, whose 1986 study Murray

Sperber cites as indicating that "football and basketball players were 38% more likely to be implicated in such crimes than the average male college student." Similar statistics have been noted among high schoolers. Even when they are not physically abusive, male athletes may have trouble relating to women on an adult level. One symptom of that trouble is the attitude many of them display toward women reporters.

Until the 1970s, women sports reporters were a rarity. Those few women who did try to break into what had always been considered a man's field found themselves working at a disadvantage. For instance, team coaches and managers allowed men, but not women, to conduct postgame interviews with male athletes. Such interviews, carried out only after players have had from five to seven minutes to cool down and duck in and out of the shower, are popular among readers, and getting them is important in furthering a reporter's career. Charging that the no-women-in-the-locker-room rule injured them professionally and financially, women reporters filed an antibias suit. They won their case in a 1978 federal court ruling.

Some men in sports are still having trouble with that ruling. Two incidents in particular marred the NFL's 1990–91 season. In one, Cincinnati Bengals coach Sam Wyche kept a female reporter from entering his team's locker room. In the other, three New England Patriots players taunted a Boston newswoman with obscene remarks and behavior as she waited for an after-game interview. In both instances, NFL commissioner Paul Tagliabue imposed fines—$5,000 on each of two Patriots players, $12,500 on the third, and $50,000 on the club itself. In addition, the reporter herself received a monetary out-of-court settlement from the team. For his offense, Wyche was docked a week's salary, $27,941.

The Bengals' coach (he has since left the team) responded

to the fine by announcing a crusade aimed at getting female reporters out of locker rooms for good. His antiwoman stance runs contrary to a fundamental assumption of modern sport—that it is democratic in nature. As much as a gambling fix or an athlete's use of a performance-enhancer, sexism violates one of sport's ethical underpinnings. Yet Wyche has plenty of company. In 1991, one U.S. sports promoter was making plans for a so-called professional women's basketball league whose players would wear "form-fitting" spandex unitards "required to be attractive." *Sports Illustrated* may laud outstanding female athletes, but its editors also cling to the tradition of their annual "swimsuit issue." The baseball teams that hire ball girls to work alongside their ball boys retrieving foul balls and doing clubhouse chores don't expect the girls to be as strong or as athletic as the boys. They do, however, expect them to wear outfits that, unlike the boys' uniforms, feature tight shorts. A token four women were hired to umpire in minor-league baseball in the 1980s. Not one was promoted to the majors.

While sport has been discriminating against women, it's been doing the same to blacks and members of other minority groups. Although racial separation in sport may not date back to primitive times—racially mixed societies being a more recent phenomenon—it's safe to say that separations based on family or tribal status have. Human beings are amazingly creative about inventing so-called reasons to set themselves up as superior to other human beings. Similarly, while the later European laws that reserved certain leisure activities to the rich and noble were not racially motivated, they did reflect the usual ruling-class urge to find ways of maintaining its own wealth and status at someone else's expense. In America, that urge has found its most frequent and repugnant outlet in discrimination based on skin color.

Racism has been a fact of American life since the earliest European explorers began mistreating the New World peoples they "discovered" along with America at the end of the fifteenth century. Africans were imported as slaves into the colonies as early as 1619, and slavery continued to exist for 246 years thereafter. Although it became illegal after 1865, law and custom enforced racial separation in virtually every aspect of life. Allen Guttmann does list a few nineteenth-century black athletes—boxer Tom Molineaux, who went thirty-three rounds against an English champion in 1810; jockeys Oliver Lewis and Isaac Murphy, Kentucky Derby winners in the late 1800s; a handful of football players—but their numbers were tiny.

So was the number of early twentieth-century black or minority-group sports figures. There were Jack Johnson and Joe Lewis in boxing and track star Jesse Owens, winner of four Gold Medals at the 1936 Olympics. There were the men of the Negro baseball leagues—men like pitcher Satchel Paige and James "Cool Papa" Bell. Blacks did not appear on pro basketball teams, although the agile and entertaining Harlem Globetrotters were permitted to amuse crowds waiting for the real action to get underway. And Jim Thorpe, a 1912 Olympic contender whose Native American mother was a member of the Sac tribe, played briefly with the baseball Giants in 1919. But that was about it. In 1867, the National Association of Base Ball Players had voted to refuse to admit "any club which may be composed of one or more colored persons," and baseball set the tone for other sports. Over the next eighty years, the national pastime provided a pathway into mainstream America for succeeding generations of newcomers to the United States: first, for players of Irish descent—John McGraw, Joe McGinnity, then of German—Honus Wagner, George Herman Ruth, and later of Italian—

Yogi Berra, Joe DiMaggio. But not until April 15, 1947, did changing racial attitudes and the beginnings of the modern civil rights movement give the Brooklyn Dodgers the courage to send Jackie Robinson to bat at Ebbets Field.

By then, other sports were integrating as well. Pro football signed its first black players in 1946. Four years later, the Boston Celtics became the first NBA team to offer a contract to a black man. Althea Gibson reigned as America's first great black tennis star in the late 1950s and Arthur Ashe as its second a decade later. Blacks shone in track and field. Today they, and other nonwhites as well, are visible throughout sport. They are far, however, from being fully integrated into it.

In the first place, blacks are not distributed evenly in sport. They are well represented in basketball and football. Over-represented even: 60 percent of NFL players are black as compared to 12.1 percent of the general population. Blacks are much less common in golf, tennis, and skating. And how many black yachtsmen are there? The dearth of minorities in sports that call for expensive equipment or spacious surroundings can be explained to some extent by economics. Generally, blacks are more likely than whites to live in or near poverty and away from well-to-do suburbs with their elaborate sports facilities. But the lack of darker faces is also due to overt racism. It was racism that, right into the 1990s, routinely led PGA officials to schedule tournament events on courses at country clubs that refused to admit blacks as guests or members. It was, says football star Raghib Ismail, a blatantly racist crack from a New England Patriots team executive that clinched his decision to sign with the Canadian Football League instead of the NFL in 1991. The executive had commented scathingly about Ismail's intelligence as a black man.

Even when blacks are present on a team's bench or in its clubhouse, they are not necessarily equally represented on the playing field. Guttmann points to mathematical analyses demonstrating that blacks tend to fill "peripheral" rather than "central" playing positions. "Peripheral" refers to positions that allow for less frequent player interaction than "central" ones. Running backs and outfielders are considered peripheral; quarterbacks and catchers central.

What science suggests, observation confirms. The scarcity of black quarterbacks in the NFL is notorious. Former Washington Redskin Doug Williams, one of the few blacks who has held a quarterback position, is openly bitter about some aspects of his NFL experience. Pro teams hesitate to risk playing a black quarterback as a starter, he charges: "Most NFL coaches, general managers and owners are . . . afraid if they play a black quarterback and he doesn't pan out, they're going to be ridiculed by their peers." Furthermore, few owners are willing to pay quarterback wages—as a rule, the highest in the game—to a black. As a starting player in 1982, Williams adds, his salary was only $120,000. "That was the 54th-highest salary for NFL quarterbacks. Everybody's backup was making more than me."

The discrimination does more than turn black high school quarterbacks into college and professional running backs. It helps keep blacks out of coaching and managing jobs. Another study cited by Guttmann shows that although only 36 percent of football playing positions are defined as central, "65 percent of all NCAA Division I head coaches and 49 percent of the assistant coaches had occupied these positions in their college days." In other words, a central position is a good jumping-off place for a lucrative postplaying career. A peripheral one is not. So not only are most black players relegated to inferior and less well paid positions on-field than most white players, but they are also less apt than whites to end up coaching or managing once their playing days are over. Much less apt. According to Murray Sperber, a 1987 study revealed that at 278 Division I schools, blacks accounted for only 4.2 percent of head coaches in football, basketball, baseball, and men's track. Just 3.1 percent of assistants were black.

There are other depressing statistics. Between August 1990 and September 1991, says Claire Smith, major-league baseball hired eleven general managers, three club presidents, and eight field managers. *One* of the twenty-two was black— and that despite a deliberate campaign by some baseball officials to see to it that more minorities get front-office jobs. The owners of the NL's new Denver franchise, the Colorado Rockies, did not so much as interview a single black or Hispanic individual for an executive position, much less hire one, even though they had publicly pledged a front-office racial mix. League president Bill White, himself a black, and then-commissioner Fay Vincent, who is white, expressed outrage at the broken promise. In the press box, too, minorities are underrepresented. According to 1991 figures from the National Association of Black Journalists, America's 1,611 daily newspapers employed only five black sports columnists along with what *New York Times* sportswriter William Rhoden characterized as "a handful" of black football reporters. The *Times*'s Richard Sandomir complained that network television broadcasts of football games between black colleges are "rare enough to be never." One New England businessman and former state legislator noted that at the 1991 Boston Red Sox home opener, "The small army of hustlers (or vendors) selling hotdogs, etc. . . . were all young men with white faces." Apparently even the least glamorous of jobs are saved for whites at Fenway Park.

Is there reason to hope that sport will change its racial balance to more accurately reflect its theoretical commitment to fairness? Again, the signals are confused. The Rockies made a promise and reneged on it. Baseball waited until 1991 to honor the black athletes of the old Negro Leagues, but honor them it eventually did in a ceremony that year at its Hall of Fame. The 1990s also saw the success of a decades-long effort by athletes from around the world to help do away with one extreme form of racism. Thanks in part to pressure from sports organizations, the nation of South Africa was at last starting to dismantle its system of apartheid, the strict segregation of the races.

South Africa had adopted its racist policies in 1948. Under apartheid as it applied to athletics, no South African black was allowed to compete with or against any white player. During the 1960s, a number of international athletic associations protested the system by refusing to compete against South African teams and players. The IOC joined the boycott in 1970, and over the next twenty years South Africa was formally banned from the Olympics. Finally, the South African government began taking steps to end apartheid. With that, the IOC issued an invitation to its 1992 Summer Games.

South Africa responded by fielding racially integrated teams. The change meant real progress in race relations, and sport had done its part to help bring that change about. Yet there is more to the story. Over the years of the boycott, thousands of individual athletes did appear in sporting events with South African teams and players. Of those who violated the agreement, most were from the United States.

In other ways, too, American sport's racial future is unclear. In 1990, football commissioner Tagliabue announced his intention of taking Super Bowl XXVII, set for 1993 in Phoenix, Arizona, away from that city. As a state, Arizona refused to observe the federal holiday in honor of black civil rights leader Martin Luther King, Jr. Sixty percent of NFL players are black, and Tagliabue thought it an insult to them to schedule their championship event in Phoenix. NFL owners agreed. In 1992, Arizona voters did decide to honor the King holiday. On the other hand, when the NFL's Washington Redskins team came under pressure from Native American groups to change its racist-sounding name to something less offensive, team owners refused. Owners and officials on other teams, and in other sports, have likewise resisted giving up names, mascots, and symbols that Native Americans see as demeaning to themselves.

More ambiguities abound. In 1991, executives at NBC-TV experimented with black college football, broadcasting a game between Grambling State and Southern University. But NBC made it plain that if viewership did not meet expectations, black college football was out. Mixed news comes from golf, too, with private country clubs in many parts of the country clinging to discriminatory whites-only (and in some instances, men-only) membership rules. On the other hand, after pro golf sponsors Honda, Toyota, IBM, and Anheuser-Busch threatened to withdraw their corporate backing for the game unless the PGA stopped scheduling events at whites-only courses, the association announced an end to its seventy-four-year history of condoning segregated play.

Public relations ploy? Or genuine commitment to change? Only time will tell. And only time will tell how committed sport is to resolving any of its other problems either.

Chapter 6

Amateurism: Ideal or Evil?

Amateurs? What are they doing in a book about the business of sport? Amateur athletics has nothing to do with profit and loss columns. Amateurs play for the love of the game and nothing more. Why, the very word "amateur" comes from the Latin *amator,* lover. Unlike professional sport, amateur sport exists apart from any thought of monetary gain.

Or does it? Definitely not, say observers like sportswriter Leonard Koppett and Indiana University's Murray Sperber. As they see it, most sports programs we think of as amateur are as deeply concerned with money as any professional sports undertaking. So much, say Koppett and Sperber, for myth number one of amateur athletics.

Myth number two—that amateurism as we think of it has roots going back thousands of years to the original Olympic Games—is equally misleading, sports historians agree. There was nothing amateur about the Greek contenders who gathered at the arena in Elis for the first quadrennial games in 776 B.C. They were not there for the love of sport, but to fulfill a religious obligation. Each athlete was sponsored by a city, charged with devoting his play to the gods and winning their blessings—in the very material form of good harvests and rich trade—for its people. Winners received only symbolic honors at the games themselves, but once they returned home, they could count on rewards of rich prizes from their grateful fellow citizens.

No more amateur than the ancient Olympians were the long-ago warriors who developed wrestling and boxing into elaborately ritualized games. They, and later the tournament knights of medieval Europe, played with the deadly serious goal of improving the battle skills by which they survived and prospered. And there was nothing amateur in our sense of the word—unpaid, but skilled and organized—about village football or a game like rounders. Not, in fact, until the last half of the nineteenth century did our notion of sports amateurism appear. It is no coincidence that the concept emerged along with the first stirrings of professionalism in baseball and other sports.

Where did our ideas about amateurism come from? In part, they originated on midnineteenth-century English and American college campuses. The students who organized this country's first intercollegiate crew races and rugby games really could be called amateurs. Young gentlemen from well-to-do families, as were most college students of the day, they had a taste for sport and the time and money to indulge that taste while living comfortably and completing their educations. University officials, for their part, looked upon athletics as a pleasant and healthful way for students to let off steam and fill in spare time. Since administrators regarded sport as an activity apart from the main purpose of college, student-athletes were left free to assemble their own teams and manage them as they saw fit.

Ideas about amateurism were rooted as well in the newly popular nonteam sports of the later 1800s. Games like modern golf and tennis required generous, elaborately laid out spaces and expensive equipment based on the latest technology, and play was automatically limited to those who had access to courts and courses and could afford to outfit themselves with the newest in balls, racquets, clubs, and special clothing. Like privileged college athletes, these enthusiasts—many of them independently wealthy and unburdened by having to work for a living—could spend long hours playing for their own enjoyment. Not for them the kind of commercialism they saw creeping into the more commonplace game of baseball in the 1870s. Golf and tennis players were the aristocrats of sport, lovers of athletic endeavor for its own sake. That love, that spirit of amateurism, as they were beginning to call it, made their kind of sport better—purer, more high-minded—than anything smacking of paid professionalism. Or so they thought, and that thought became the third myth of amateur athletics.

Myth firmed into policy with the 1896 revival of the ancient Olympic Games. Perhaps the leader of the modern Olympic movement, the French baron Pierre de Coubertin, misunderstood the spiritual—and practical—aspects of the original games. Perhaps he was simply romanticizing history as Albert Spalding had done with Abner Doubleday and his so-called invention of baseball. In any case, de Coubertin envisioned the new games as vehicles for displaying amateur athletic talent, the epitome of sport for sport's sake. As traditionally defined by the International Olympic Committee, an amateur athlete is one who "participates and always has participated in sport as an avocation without material gain of any kind." It is a definition that has been described as everything from an "ideal" (by the IOC) to "poisonous hypocrisy" and "evil *in principle*" (by Leonard Koppett). Doubtless the truth lies somewhere between the two extremes, but this much seems clear: the nineteenth-century concept of amateurism is incompatible with the nature of modern sport.

To understand why, think of baseball. By the IOC definition,

America's earliest baseball players were amateurs, adults who still loved a childhood game and played it with no thought of pleasing anyone but themselves. Nevertheless, when their games began attracting public spectators, the attention was not unwelcome. Neither, when the spectators proved willing to pay admission, was their money. Nor did players refuse money when it was offered by backers in the business community. Why should they? Few of them were privileged college kids or men of independent means. They were hardworking farmers and clerks and factory hands who not only had to support themselves, but also had to find the money for such extras as uniforms and equipment. If fans were willing to contribute toward those extras, why not let them?

And if the contributions were generous enough to leave something over for the players, so much the better. Not only did the new income benefit them personally by making their lives a little easier, it benefited them as athletes—and as members of a team. With a bit of cash to spare, players could take time off from their regular jobs to hone their baseball skills. Greater skill meant higher-quality play. Higher-quality play meant much more public interest and more paying spectators, and that in turn meant fresh money and still more time for practice. Team play grew increasingly sophisticated.

So did baseball itself. As teams went openly pro and started offering wages to players, they were able to tap into a larger pool of talent. Physically adept young men from the nation's poor and middle-income families far outnumbered its rich, upper-class athletes, and hundreds of would-be stars who could never have afforded to join an amateur club were eager to try for places on the play-for-pay outfits. Those who won them brought new skill and energy to the game. Over the decades, they used both to refine and reconstruct the sport, eventually transforming the crude "town game" of the 1840s and 1850s into America's graceful national pastime. It was a transformation that would not have been possible had baseball insisted upon sticking to its amateur status. Baseball prospered as a modern sport, democratically aware that its best players were not necessarily its richest and that there is nothing vulgar about paying athletes to do what they most love doing. As time passed, other sports—football, hockey, basketball—recognized these same truths and prospered likewise.

Sports like track and field, tennis, and golf, on the other hand, seemed determined to cling to their amateur "ideal." So doing, they reflected the spirit of the medieval laws that had kept "upper-class" games off-limits to ordinary men and women. Until well into the 1900s, U.S. golf's leading matches were closed to nonamateurs. Then, in 1916, the Professional Golfers Association was organized and its members, many of them country club golfing instructors, began agitating for the opportunity to compete at those matches. By the 1920s, golf officials had bowed to their demands, and pros and amateurs were playing together in "open" competition. Although some players of the day, Bobby Jones, for instance, were lifelong amateurs, spectator golf was to all intents and purposes a professional sport by the 1930s.

Tennis was a more stubborn holdout. The game's first pro player organization, the U.S. Professional Lawn Tennis Association, was founded in 1927. It put together a profitable tour, but failed in its bids to get into such amateur classics as Wimbledon or Davis Cup play. The failure left talented but not-rich competitors with a choice. They could turn professional and support themselves decently on the pro tour. If they did, they had to forgo the game's most prestigious events and face snubs from "real" sportsmen and women. Or they could maintain their precious amateur standing and eke out a living teaching their game or by accepting quiet gifts of cash, jewelry, and other valuables from rich fans. Following the latter course gave them entry into the game's highest echelons—but it also earned them a distasteful label: "kept players." Not until 1968, when the International Tennis Association opened up to the pros, was the players' dilemma resolved. With the most skilled players spicing up the most important events, tennis flourished.

Track and field reacted to the pressure to democratize—professionalize—differently. In theory, the sport is still amateur, its competitors forbidden by the International Amateur Athletic Federation (IAAF) to receive direct recompense for their athletic endeavors. However, under IAAF rules, players may sign contracts to endorse commercial products. They may also accept fees for showing up at certain invitational events. The stratagems allow both athletes and the IAAF to claim amateur status while at the same time ensuring that the world's best players will be on hand to keep the competition interesting.

Even the IOC, the body responsible for coming up with the definition of amateurism in its strictest form, has had to modify that definition. At one time, the Olympic standard was absolute. So absolute, in fact, that after the 1912 Games, IOC officials forced American Jim Thorpe, who had left the Games with the decathlon gold medal, to surrender his honor. Why? Because Thorpe had played semiprofessional baseball with a North Carolina team a few years earlier. (It was not until after the 1912 Olympics that Thorpe would join the fully professional New York Giants.) What has semipro ball to do with the broad jump, the shot put, or the 200-meter dash? Not much. It was the fact that Thorpe had once exchanged his athletic services for money that outraged IOC sensibilities. In 1982, the committee at last reversed itself, voting to give the medal back to Thorpe (who had at that point been dead for almost three decades). Even now, *The World Almanac* lists the 1912 decathlon champion as Sweden's Hugo Wieslander, with 7,724.49 points. Only a fine-print footnote records Thorpe's 8,413 score, 688.51 points higher than Wieslander's. So much for past IOC commitment to the fair play and meaningful records supposed to be so central to modern sport.

More recent Olympic officials, though, have gone a long way toward reconciling the amateur "ideal" with athletic reality. A 1974 rules change permits Olympic contenders to be provided with paid jobs and receive expense money during unlimited months of training. For U.S. Olympic hopefuls, the new rule may mean being hired to work for a sponsoring corporation. Along with paying the athlete a salary, corporate bosses arrange a schedule flexible enough to allow for ample practice time. Beyond that, the IOC has opened some of its events, including ice hockey, soccer, and tennis to the pros. In 1992, the National Basketball Association sent its first team to the Summer Olympics in Barcelona, Spain. It's taken most of a century, but the IOC, like the ITA, the IAAF, and other sports associations, is finally recognizing that professionalism in sport is nothing to be ashamed of and that athletes are no more able than anyone else to live without visible means of support.

That leaves college sports. Among the first to field amateur teams, expert and structured, but unpaid and part-time, colleges and universities like to pretend they are still sending such teams out to play today. The pretense has people like Leonard Koppett and Murray Sperber crying foul.

Let's see why. College athletics changed as rapidly as anything else in sport in the late nineteenth century. By the 1880s, U.S. students had invented American football. Within twenty years, it and basketball were wildly popular on—and off—

campus. To the surprise of college administrators, winning teams attracted not just student spectators but the general public as well and could earn a school enormous prestige. At some colleges and state universities, sport went quickly from being a pleasant extra to assuming a central role in defining that school and giving it its distinctive image.

As a defining asset, sport was too valuable to leave in student hands, and college athletes—like the baseball players of the 1870s—began seeing their games taken away from them. In baseball, those doing the taking had been entrepreneurs-turned-owner. At the colleges, it was the university that assumed the position of owner. Here, too, capital separated itself from labor, and, as in baseball, that capital was used to hire professional trainers, coaches, and others whose job it was to run a team on a daily basis. At "big-sports" schools, athletic bureaucracies grew large and powerful. In 1906, college sport borrowed again from baseball, duplicating its league structure in the National Collegiate Athletic Association. Over time, the NCAA took on responsibility for overseeing the sports programs of member schools, issuing and enforcing rules about the recruitment of high school athletes, student eligibility, play and practice policies, coaching duties and responsibilities, and so on. In only one way did college sport differ from the professional kind: its players were not paid.

Not at the start, anyway. But college sport, like baseball, captured first the public's interest—then its money. As in baseball, that money, initially spent on the team as a whole, began gravitating toward individual players. Again, why not? America's twentieth-century student population was not made up almost exclusively of rich young men; much of it was of middle- or working-class origin. The sons of auto mechanics and grocery store clerks were no better able to afford sport for sport's sake than were the earliest professional baseball players. Joining a school team might even mean having to sacrifice the part-time job that enabled many a collegian to pay for his education. If needy students were going to be on a team (and if they were athletically talented that was exactly where sports-oriented college officials wanted them), someone would have to make it up to them financially for time spent in play and practice.

So colleges began offering athletic scholarships—small ones to begin with, just enough to allow a poor boy to stay in school and play for its team. Then, as college sport boomed and money poured in from radio and television, scholarships grew. Today, says Murray Sperber, big-sports schools like the University of Kansas and Oklahoma State average $3.7 million annually in athletic scholarships. Stanford University in California shells out about $5 million a year. And that's only what is officially reported to the NCAA. Sperber contends that many schools quietly make additional grants to athletes out of general university funds. For athletes, those grants add up to a good deal: the cost of a four-year education. From Sperber's point of view, they add up to a professional salary.

Athletic scholarships constitute a salary, Sperber argues, because they are dependent upon athletic performance. Under the NCAA rules of twenty years ago, athletic scholarships, once granted, could not be revoked. Even if a recipient did not play up to expectations—even if he quit the team—his scholarship would still be paid, giving him the chance to finish school and graduate. That rule was dropped in 1973. "Under pressure from coaches who wanted greater control over their players and the ability to 'fire' them for poor athletic performances," Sperber writes, "the NCAA instituted one-year scholarships, renewed annually at the athletic department's discretion. . . . If the athlete . . . quits the team, the institution withdraws the financial package." No play, no pay. That sounds plenty professional to Sperber: "Under their current terms," he says, "athletic scholarships appear indistinguishable from what the IRS [Internal Revenue Service, the federal income tax collection agency] calls 'barter payment for services rendered,' thus making college athletes professional wage earners." Ira Berkow of the *New York Times* agrees. "Colleges hire players to come to school to play sports," he states flatly, ". . . and everyone in the world knows it."

Moreover, athletic scholarships are only one type of compensation offered players at big-sports schools, Sperber continues. Anyone curious about some of the other kinds should consult his 1990 book, *College Sports, Inc.* Even the table of contents is revealing. Chapter twenty-nine promises to tell readers "How Athletic Departments Pay On-Campus Athletes: Cash, Free Loans, Jobs for Jocks, Hard & Soft Tickets," while chapter thirty tackles "Athletes' Legal & Illegal Perks: Jock Dorms, Fast Cars, Free Credit Cards, & Free Phone Calls Home & to a Bail Bondsman."

The two chapters make for compelling reading. According to Sperber, it is accepted practice for wealthy fans to give their favorite athletes generous cash handouts. "Sugar daddy boosters," these fans are called. Their paybacks: choice seats at game time and the chance to hobnob with the stars. The cash-ticket transfers are discreetly managed by members of a team's professional coaching staff. As former NFLer Calvin Hill remembers the college experience of another player, that player "never met his sugar daddy . . . Every Monday, he [the player] would go to a safe-deposit box and pick up his ticket money . . . An assistant coach took care of giving the sugar daddy the tickets." Both player and coach were breaking NCAA rules; cash payoffs have no place in the kind of amateurism that college sport claims to represent. NCAA officials, anxious to defend their programs, call sugar daddy deals rare. Sperber begs to differ. "Contrary to NCAA propaganda," he quotes one sociologist as reporting, "illegal payments are not isolated incidents but constitute a flourishing 'underground economy' in college sports."

The Indiana professor gets plenty of confirmation from the headlines as well. During the fall of 1991, sports reports were full of news about former Auburn University football player Eric Ramsey, who secretly tape-recorded three years' worth of conversations with his coach at the Alabama school. The tapes revealed that Ramsey had received regular cash handouts—and that the coach knew it. In December 1991, Dexter Cambridge of the University of Texas was declared ineligible for play after taking $7,000 from a booster. Two months later, a basketball player at the University of Nevada at Las Vegas (UNLV) came under fire when he broke NCAA rules by allowing a university employee to bail him out of jail after an arrest. NCAA athletes are supposed to post their own bail money.

Illegal bailouts, surreptitious bonuses, and pay-for-play scams disguised as athletic scholarships are far from being the only graft Sperber and other critics find in university athletic departments. At some schools, coaches and ADs begin paying young athletes off before they even join the college team.

It's been over forty years since the NCAA adopted rules governing the recruitment of high school players by college coaches. Broadly speaking, the rules are aimed at making sure colleges treat eager, often naive, young players fairly and honestly. Coaches are not supposed to offer high school prospects cash payments to sign on with their departments, for example. They are not supposed to promise them favored treatment in college nor to entertain them lavishly while they make their college decisions.

It's that last rule, the one about no lavish entertaining, that's most frequently ignored, according to the NCAA's own reckoning. Colleges and universities encourage prospective college athletes, like other prospective college students, to visit their campuses as high school seniors. Unlike ordinary seniors, though, top athletes may be transported to the campus, along with their parents, their brothers and sisters—even their girlfriends—at university expense. The university athletic department may also foot the bill for hotel rooms, meals, and a night out on the town. All more or less within the rules, although there are limits. Definitely against the rules are extra gifts of money, goods, or services, but at schools hungry for top talent, such gifts are made. Also against the rules are promises about luxury dormitories for athletes, free cars, "jobs" that consist mostly of pay and hardly at all of work, and so on. But as many as 65 percent of Division I coaches make them. Others offer outright bribes. Basketball's John Williams, charged in 1985 with point shaving at Tulane University before signing with the Cleveland Cavaliers, confessed to having accepted $10,000 to enroll at Tulane.

Recruitment violations underline another inconsistency in college sport's claim to be an amateur affair of student-athletes. There is very little of the student about a great many of the athletes so eagerly pursued by big-sports schools. In 1990, UNLV faced charges of having signed up one basketball prospect who never managed to graduate from his New York City high school. The recruit played brilliant ball—and read on a second-grade level. Tulane's John Williams arrived at college with combined Scholastic Aptitude Test (SAT) scores of under 500. Since the minimum combined score is 400, and the maximum 1,600, the inference has to be that the school wanted Williams for reasons having little to do with academics.

Once at college, many big-time student-athletes continue
to shy away from learning. How could they do otherwise,
with schedules of as many as twenty-seven basketball games
and up to thirty hours a week devoted to games and practice?
Thirty hours a week is, NCAA officials admit, more than college athletes spend in classroom and study combined. "Not
more than 20 percent of the football players go to college for
an education," comments Jim Walden, head football coach at
Iowa State. "And that may be a high figure." For black athletes, at least, it is. Tennis's Arthur Ashe cites statistics indicating that of the 10,000 or so black football and basketball
players on athletic scholarships as the 1990s began, only
18 percent could be expected to graduate.

But ADs make mighty efforts to buttress the fiction that
players are getting an education. "Most big-time athletic programs," Sperber says, try to get around the no-time-to-learn
problem by having students "major in eligibility" to meet
NCAA academic standards, which he labels "minimal." Athletes are directed toward easy "gut" courses, for example.
When a player flunks even that sort of course, fiction may
yet triumph over fact. John Williams failed one psychology
course three times without losing either his scholarship or his
eligibility. Some ADs persuade teachers to inflate athletes'
grades. Others conspire to get those grades altered or to see
credit given for courses not taken.

Having taken the "student" out of "student-athlete," some
coaches go on to treat their players like the professionals they
truly are—callously. Like pros, college athletes face the risk
of injury or worse. Loyola Marymount University basketball
star Hank Gathers suffered a heart attack and died during a
1990 championship play-off game. He died knowing of his
heart condition—he had suffered a mild attack earlier—knowing also that he was not on proper medication for that con-

dition. Why wasn't he? Because Gathers—and his coach and the team doctor—agreed that the medicine prescribed for him after his first attack was slowing him down. With Loyola Marymount in national contention, Gathers *had* to play at his best. Doctor and coach cut his dosage. Gathers never did get his shot at NBA fame and fortune. Brendan Kinney, a junior-college football star recruited by Cornell University, used the pages of the *New York Times* to list a few of his playing injuries: "13 concussions, a separated shoulder, a torn rotator cuff, severely torn muscles in my back and legs, sprained ankles, knees, and elbows, broken fingers and toes, and innumerable abrasions and cuts." Unlike Gathers, Kinney was never encouraged to play with a potentially life-threatening condition. But he did feel "forced" to play with an accumulation of injuries that ended his career before he got to don a Cornell uniform.

Besides threatening their playing futures and cheating many of them academically, the critics go on, college athletic departments gyp their players financially. Financially? By Murray Sperber's estimate, a big-time college football or basketball star gets anywhere from $5,000 to $20,000 a year in cash and freebies. That's a lot of money.

It's also a lot less than he would be earning in the NFL or the NBA. John Williams may have picked up $10,000, a scholarship, and who knows what else before he got to Tulane, but when he left, the Cleveland Cavaliers handed him $675,000. From $20,000-odd a year to roughly thirty-four times that is quite a jump in pay. Yet Williams was as much a professional athlete—someone who is paid in return for playing—at Tulane as with the Cavaliers. Calling him an amateur, while playing him as a professional, saved Tulane's athletic department a bundle.

It may have been a bundle Tulane, in common with a lot

of other schools, needed to save. "One of the best-kept secrets about intercollegiate athletics," says Murray Sperber, "is that most college sports programs lose money." Most? "Of the 802 members of the NCAA" and some 1,500-odd non-NCAA schools, Sperber claims, "only 10 to 20 athletic programs make a consistent albeit small profit." About twenty or thirty others break even. "The rest—over 2,300 institutions—lose anywhere from a few dollars to millions annually." One NCAA official estimated the University of Michigan's athletic department losses for 1988–89 at $2.5 million. By 1993, the school's yearly sports deficit was expected to double.

Such deficits seem impossible, given all we read and hear about billion-dollar television contracts and college teams getting millions more for tournament and bowl appearances. But what the public sees and hears isn't necessarily the whole story. Instead of sharing all its TV money with member schools, the NCAA keeps over half itself. Schools selected for bowl games, on the other hand, are required to split their earnings evenly with other members of their conference. In a ten-member conference, $1 million shrinks to $100,000 mighty fast. "In addition," says Sperber, "athletic departments like to turn bowl and tournament trips into all-expenses-paid junkets for hundreds of people, including their employees and friends. Their travel, hotel, and entertainment costs often eat up the actual bowl or tourney payouts and transform post-season play into a deficit item!" So how do ADs come up with the cash to run their programs? Sperber's answer: "From their schools' general operating funds and other university sources." Only by "fudging" their arithmetic and resorting to such stratagems as disguising athletic scholarships as some other form of financial aid do big-sports schools appear to operate at a profit. And that is despite the fact that government regards college sports programs as part of an institution's "educational mission" and therefore does not tax them.

Are college "amateurs" aware they are being used—and abused—as professionals? Some are. And they're doing something about it: leaving school and turning pro, the way Raghib Ismail did when he dropped out of Notre Dame to join the Canadian Football League in 1991. Why should the Rocket have settled for $20,000 a year running and carrying with the Fighting Irish when he could be pulling down close to $4 million for doing the same job with another team?

Sad to say, the transition from college to contract doesn't go as smoothly for everyone as it did for Ismail. NFL and NBA rules do allow players to declare for the professional draft while still in college, and the World League of American Football once considered drafting high school players. However, NCAA rules say that once a player enters the pro draft, he loses his amateur ranking for good and is no longer eligible for a college team. That's no problem for a declared player if—and it's a big if—some professional team signs him up. But those who go unsigned—twenty out of thirty-eight in the NFL's 1990 draft alone—can no longer play at an NCAA school. Their lack of eligibility robs them of their scholarships (no play, no pay) and for a lot of college athletes—many from families unable to begin to pay college tuition bills— the withdrawal of a scholarship spells an end to school. "He was one semester from graduating with an English degree," mourned the mother of a Notre Dame running back bypassed in the NFL draft. "I'm 12 hours short of a degree in health promotion," said a Vanderbilt junior who found himself in the same boat. "I'm one semester short of getting a degree in economics," according to a third who gambled and lost on the draft. In 1990, a Notre Dame junior who failed in the NFL draft took the NCAA to court in an effort to regain his amateur standing. He lost his case.

Then there are those who lose out by putting their chips on staying in school and earning a degree. Mississippi junior

Gerald Glass was one. Faced with the option of entering the 1988 NFL draft—where the guessing was he'd be a top pick—Glass decided on graduation. He wound up twentieth pick in 1989, with a poorer contract than he almost certainly would have had the year before. His example would do little to inspire an indecisive junior to remain in school. Additional pressure to select the draft over graduation originates in the ever-present fear of a college injury that could put an end to any hope of a pro career. Still more has to do with pro football's and basketball's repeated threats to impose salary caps on draftees. That threat, and the players' resulting conviction that they had better get what they can while they can, "has done more than anything else to flush underclassmen out of college," *Sports Illustrated* charges.

What has the NCAA been doing about problems like the financial and academic exploitation of college athletes and the corruption in big-sports programs? Not enough, its critics say. NCAA officials did make a 1990 promise that they would consider allowing underclassmen who declare for the pro draft but are not chosen by a team to get back their college eligibility. The promise made, the subject dropped out of the spotlight. Taking its place was the story of how NCAA officials dealt with the scandal-ridden Syracuse University basketball program in 1991. According to Syracuse news reports, several players had accepted booster money, autos, and other illicit goodies. One had had his grades changed so he could keep on playing. University officials looked into the allegations and found them to be true. They suspended the seven players involved and announced that the Syracuse team would play its next game—a televised matchup with Notre Dame—using players scrounged from the bench, from the school's football team, from wherever they could be located.

Oh no you don't! replied the NCAA, reinstating the seven

on the spot. As Ira Berkow explained it, "The NCAA has a television contract and it must surely provide the best entertainment possible, and it would not brook a team with some walk-on football players . . . Sponsors, after all, are paying good money for the best video product." It should not surprise anyone if players and coaches at Syracuse—and at every other college with a lucrative television sports contract—feel they can count on the NCAA's blessing while flouting NCAA rules. Even when the NCAA does penalize a sports program, that punishment may miss its mark. For recruitment violations that occurred in the 1970s, the UNLV basketball team was banned from NCAA television and tournament play in 1991–92. That meant UNLV players were being penalized (and it was a serious penalty—pro scouts watch tournament play with the draft in mind) for wrongs committed by their coaches and others when the players themselves were infants or toddlers. Why must team members suffer for the misdeeds of others? Because, says sportswriter Allen Barra, "athletes are easier to punish than coaches and administrators; they have no rights."

Aware of the criticisms aimed in their direction, some college athletics authorities have begun thinking about reform. A policy adopted by the CFA in 1986 requires academically deficient recruits at sixty top football schools to spend their freshman years studying rather than playing. By 1992, adherence to that policy had contributed to a 12 percent increase in graduation rates among football players, from just under 52 percent earning their degrees in 1990 to a little over 57 percent doing so two years later.

But other proposed reforms seem less likely to bring about real change. At its January 1991 national convention, the NCAA announced a series of new rules aimed at quelling criticism of its programs. Mandatory team practice times would be reduced. "Jock dorms" would be eliminated. Coaching staffs would be cut. There would be fewer athletic scholarships at big-sports schools. In 1992, the group voted to tighten academic standards for college athletes.

"Barely Eligible" was the headline over Murray Sperber's *New York Times* column about the rules changes, which he and other skeptics regarded as so slight as to be close to meaningless. Coaching staff cuts were limited to a single position in most cases, for example, while the number of athletic scholarships Division I schools were permitted to offer dropped from ninety-five to eighty-five in football and fifteen to thirteen in basketball. What was more, even those mild reforms were scheduled to be phased in over a period of up to five years. That margin of time allows for "additions, subtractions, compromises and concessions that some people think could dilute the effectiveness of [the] reforms," William Rhoden noted. As for NCAA pledges to put substance into the term "student-athlete," the critics say they've heard it all before. Back in 1983, the NCAA had nineteen schools on probation and thirty-five more under investigation in connection with grade inflation and grades-related recruitment violations. The investigations made news, but they produced little lasting effect. The problem with the 1992 reforms, says Rhoden, is that while they raise academic standards for athletes, they do not give the athletes any additional study time in which to work to meet those standards. If the standards cannot be met, what's to stop ADs from going right on helping athletes "major in eligibility?"

Why the NCAA resistance to genuine reform? "Money," Sperber asserts. Limiting practice time, forcing players to hit the books, and cutting coaching jobs will mean a lower quality of play. Lower quality will mean smaller television audiences. "When the ratings decline, will CBS still want to pay $1 billion to televise the NCAA basketball tournament through 1997?" Sperber wonders. And if CBS doesn't want to pay, if network executives insist upon renegotiating their contract, what happens to NCAA and college athletic department revenues?

Real reform also comes down to money in another way. That's because real reform means taking one of two courses. The first would be to return college sport to its origins, handing teams back over to their members, who would be genuine student-athletes. The second would be to go openly professional, hiring and paying players who would have no obligation ever to set foot in a classroom. Following the first course would require colleges to forgo those rich television contracts and threaten to put the NCAA out of business. Following the second would cost schools millions of dollars in team payrolls. It would place them squarely in the way of Internal Revenue Service tax collectors, too. So far, schools and the NCAA have managed to steer clear of the IRS. But let them start paying players in an openly profit-seeking venture and tax bills go straight into the mail. The prospect is not an appealing one, nor is the idea of going back to a nineteenth-century way of doing things. That is why genuine NCAA reform is, as Sperber so colorfully puts it, "about as likely as pigs slam-dunking basketballs."

NCAA attitudes—its tolerance for rule breaking, its shaky commitment to reform—have implications that go beyond college sport. They take their toll on high school—even junior high—players and programs. That's partly because younger players are influenced by what they see happening in colleges and universities. Football and basketball players especially know that the road to a big-league career has traditionally included a stop at the college level. But NCAA impact on high school sports owes far more to the fact that high school coaches are also influenced by college programs and by how they see the association dealing with them. After all, high school coaches, particularly at those schools where sports are a high priority, are preparing their best athletes to enter NCAA programs. The most successful high school coaches may even win college coaching jobs for themselves. Naturally, they tend to run their own teams along the lines established by the colleges.

So it should come as no surprise if big-time high school sports programs display some of the flaws of big-time college sports. High school "amateurs," like their university counterparts, may receive financial recompense for playing. The recompense could be a scholarship at a private high school with a strong sports program. More often, the reward for outstanding high school performance is eventual college recruitment and the university scholarship that could be a youngster's ticket to a pro career. The fact that the college grant does not come until after high school does not make its value any less real.

Other forms of "payment" may be dangled before high school athletes. Top high school basketball teams enjoy perks like invitations to national tournament play. The first national high school basketball tournament, the Holiday Prep Classic, was held in Las Vegas in 1976 and cost $3,500. In December 1989 almost three dozen high school teams traveled to Nevada to participate in a $100,000 extravaganza, one of thirty such events staged nationwide that month. Tournament players get a plane trip, lodging, food, and a dazzling vacation—paid for, in whole or in part, by organizers eager to attract the country's best teams. Players also get a thorough looking over by college scouts. Members of top high school teams can expect other material rewards, such as athletic shoes, uniforms, and warm-up suits donated by companies looking for extra exposure for their products. And there are less tangible compensations. In 1990, cable television's SportsChannel America in cooperation with the National Federation of State High School Associations was lining up corporate sponsors for weekly packages of high school football and basketball games to be broadcast to audiences of up to eight and a half million viewers. That was good news for high school athletes eager to catch the eye of college recruiters.

Television contracts, scholarships, and valuable perks are not all that high school athletes and athletic programs may have in common with their college counterparts. There can also be exploitation, some of it physical. Broken bones, strained muscles, torn ligaments—even paralysis and the occasional death—may put an end to hopes for a college athletic career, much less a professional one. Former Odessa, Texas, high school football star James "Boobie" Miles knows how it feels to have that happen. As a junior fullback for Odessa's Permian High School team, Boobie was flooded with college recruitment letters. Notre Dame, Nebraska, Houston, Texas A&M, Clemson, Texas Tech, Oklahoma, Oklahoma State, Louisiana State, Southern Methodist, Arkansas, University of California at Los Angeles—they all wanted him. Permian is a top football high school, and Boobie was a top player. Then, early in his senior year, Boobie injured his knee. When his coach insisted on sending him out to play anyway, the injury worsened. Surgery followed, but Boobie never did recover. The colleges stopped calling. The Permian team didn't suffer though. "We had a heck of a running back," one Permian coach told author H. G. Bissinger, who wrote about the Permian team in his book, *Friday Night Lights*. His teammate's availability made Boobie, in his coach's word, "expendable."

College and football are not all that Boobie Miles missed

out on. A decent high school education is another, and here, too, his high school's athletic department seems to have been taking its cue from exploitive college programs. No one at Permian seems to have given much thought to what their football hero was, or was not, doing in the classroom. Non-football-playing students at the school study biology, Bissinger tells us. Football players, concentrating on maintaining their eligibility, take a course called food science and nutrition. Meantime, at Permian, as at big-sports colleges, money that could be going into academic departments is diverted into athletic accounts. According to Bissinger, Permian administrators spent $6,750 on medical supplies for its football squad in 1988–89. Rush-order film prints of games cost $6,400. The school budgeted just $5,040 for English textbooks and supplies that year. Permian's athletic department is not unique, of course. It's just the one H. G. Bissinger chose to write about.

Finally, again like so many big-sports colleges, big-sports high schools may cheat their players financially. Boobie Miles worked hard over three seasons for the payoff—the college scholarship and exposure to NFL scouts—he'll never have. He's not the only one who's watched his expectations go down the drain. A 1991 survey conducted by the Louis Harris polling organization shows that many if not most high school athletes view their exertions on the field as a guarantee of future sporting and financial success. This is especially the case among young black athletes. While 39 percent of white high school athletes expect to win a scholarship to play in college, 59 percent of blacks expect the same. Forty-three percent of blacks see themselves making the pros. Sixteen percent of whites envision a professional future. Among both groups, the great majority are doomed to disappointment. One percent of high school players go on to play in college.

Only one in 10,000—0.0001 percent—will make it to the pros.

But for that 0.0001 percent, the struggle will be worth the effort. Million-dollar contracts . . . product-endorsement possibilities . . . fame and glory . . . And, not least of all, the feeling that at last, and for however brief a time, their athletic talent and on-field achievements are being rewarded openly and honestly.

Chapter 7

Cheers and Jeers

What is modern sport? It's hits and runs and errors, slam dunks, and a last-minute touchdown pass. It's brawls on the ice, furious volleys across the net, and a thrilling hole in one. Sport is outrageous salaries matched by equally outrageous behavior. It's records set and records broken, a soaring leap, the near impossible catch, a stunning performance by a new young star. It's elaborate equipment, familiar logos, luxurious new stadiums, and beloved old ones. It's the national anthem and peanuts and popcorn and crackerjack. Sport is advertising, $130 sneakers, and, sometimes, one dark strand in a web of murder. It's corporate sponsorship, tax write-offs, ever-expanding leagues, and virtual round-the-clock television coverage. And sport is its fans.

Above all, sport is its fans. Take them away, and what's left? No Cincinnati Red Stockings team with the money to go professional back in 1869. No one to buy National League tickets seven years later. No one to cheer on the Green Bay Packers, turning them from factory hands into serious players. No college frolics transformed by popular acclaim into million-dollar bowl games; no reason for hockey to move from the ponds of Canada to indoor arenas as far south as St. Louis, San Jose, and Los Angeles; no chance for the painstakingly devised activity called basketball to become an international obsession. Take away the fans, and there are empty stands at the racetrack and no observers on the greens; no fans means no tournament tennis, no figure skating spectaculars, no competitive gymnastics, no public triumphs of track and field. Take away its fans, and sport as we know it ceases to exist.

Could sport lose its fans? The idea seems laughable. Fans have made spectator sport a $55 billion-a-year industry in the United States. According to Associated Press estimates, fans spend about $4.2 billion on tickets to sporting events of all types each year and $2.9 billion more on extras like parking, food, and beverages. Another $6.2 billion goes for such licensed products as caps, T-shirts, and jackets. Close to $3.5 billion is bet legally at the racetrack. More is gambled away through Offtrack Betting and more still outside the law.

True fan devotion to a favorite sport knows no season limits. Preseason player trades and postseason drafts are closely scrutinized and fiercely critiqued in schools and offices and barrooms across the country. Baseball fans turn out in the thousands to watch spring training matchups. When NFL teams start practice in midsummer, hundreds of devotees may show up at each session. Beyond that, some events are drawing new fans. Minor-league baseball attracted nearly twenty-five million paid spectators in 1989, reversing four decades of declining attendance. And as we have seen, informal and traditional games and pastimes are continually being refined and reinvented to satisfy the demands of a sports-hungry public.

Americans also display enthusiasm for sport away from the playing field. Super Bowl television audiences number around 100 million. In October 1991 fifty million Americans saw the Minnesota Twins beat the Atlanta Braves in seven of the most extraordinary games ever played. Nearly 20 percent of Americans with televisions tuned into all or part of the 161 hours of

Olympic competition aired during the 1992 Summer Games. Pay-per-view sporting events also attract fans. About a million U.S. cable-equipped households paid a hefty $34.95 each to watch Evander Holyfield beat Buster Douglas in their 1990 heavyweight boxing title match. Fans pay plenty to read about sports, too. *Sports Illustrated* magazine ($2.95 a week at the newsstand in 1992) ranks sixteenth in the nation in circulation, ahead of such publications as *Newsweek* and *People*, and *SI* has successfully introduced a separate publication aimed at young sports fans. Other periodicals in the nation's top 100 include *Field & Stream, Outdoor Life, American Hunter, American Rifleman, Golf Digest, Golf,* and *Sport*.

To the kind of money Americans spend to *read* about sport, add what some of them will lay out to *own* a bit of it. Take baseball cards, the kind that used to come as a bonus with a pack of cigarettes or bubble gum. When hockey star Wayne Gretzky and his partner paid $410,000 for a Honus Wagner card in 1991, the public reaction was one of amazement. But consider the prices other cards are bringing—and how fast those prices can rise. A Nolan Ryan card worth $50 in 1986 commanded $1,100 in 1991. (This according to analysts at Beckett Publications, parent company to the hobby magazine *Baseball Card Monthly*.) The 1991 value of Gretzky's own Wagner was up from $25,000 five years earlier. A 1952 Mickey Mantle card was worth $500 in 1981 and twenty times that, $10,000, a decade later. A set of baseball cards that could be bought for $4.07 in 1952 bore a $42,000 price tag in 1990. From $4.07 to $42,000, Beckett points out, is an increase of 1,031,841 percent. By contrast, gold rose in value "only" 1,139 percent between 1952 and 1991. All in all, says Beckett's B. A. Murry, baseball card sales and purchases constitute a billion-dollar annual business. What is more, baseball-card collectors are being joined by collectors of football, basketball, hockey, boxing, horseracing, minor-league baseball, and Russian ice hockey cards. Isn't that a solid indication of fan commitment to sport?

Americans demonstrate matching eagerness to possess other kinds of sports memorabilia. A baseball bat autographed by Yankee Lou Gehrig went for $27,500 at a 1990 auction. That same year, Brooklyn Dodger fans still unreconciled to the team's move to Los Angeles paid $750 apiece for seats rescued from the borough's old Ebbets Field. A pinstriped Yankees shirt worn by Mickey Mantle in 1960 brought $110,000 in 1992. (Ironically, the most Mantle himself ever got for a season's play was $100,000.) An auction house in Kennebunk, Maine, specializes in selling golf collectibles. Even Little League team pins have become collectors' items. As fifteen-year-old Steve Jones of Natrona Heights, Pennsylvania, explained to one reporter, "Most every team that plays in a regional tournament or goes on to the [Little League] World Series brings their own pins to exchange with players from other cities or other countries." For most, the exchanges are a hobby. But not for all. "Some people actually make money off of them," Steve says. Autographs are also big sellers. A pair of basketball shoes signed by Chicago Bulls' star Michael Jordan brought $1,600 at auction, while his autographed NBA All-Star jersey went for $6,400. A baseball signed by Yankee Don Mattingly sold for around $60 in 1991; Jose Canseco's signature was priced at $45.95, and Darryl Strawberry's at $28.95. How can you tell how much *your* sports star autograph is worth? Consult the *Baseball Autograph Handbook*, which keeps collectors up to date on the value of their holdings.

Autographs, trading cards, and other artifacts aren't all that dedicated sports buffs collect. For those caught up in the whimsical world of rotisserie ball, the idea is to "collect" players in order to build a "team," which then "competes" against other "teams" in a rotisserie "league."

As Boston reporter and rotisserie fanatic Nathan Cobb tells the story, "rotiss" was invented during the winter of 1979–80 at a New York City restaurant, La Rotisserie Française. (Hence its name.) Cobb calls rotisserie ball a "fantasy" game, one in which participants create their make-believe teams (baseball teams only at first, although football and basketball fans later developed rotisserie-style leagues of their own) by pretending to draft real-life major-league players. The real players' actual statistics—games won, games lost, batting averages, home runs, runs batted in, and so on—are tabulated throughout the season by rotisserie players and scored on a point basis. If a real-life player is injured, suspended, or otherwise removed from play, so is his rotisserie counterpart. "Standings are calculated weekly, with [rotisserie] teams ranked according to performance in each category," Cobb says. The imaginary teams (many with such fanciful names as the Danzig Bears, the Wonderboys, and the Borscht Belters) move up and down in the standings the way real teams do. And money is an incentive in rotiss just as it is in the real game. "All leagues collect fees from their owners for players who are 'bought' at an annual April draft," says Cobb, "and the booty goes to the first four finishers at the end of the season." The league in which he plays imposes a draft limit of $46 per owner. A more typical limit is $260, but there are rotisserie players for whom money—lots of money—is the main point of playing. "Some leagues are little more than gambling operations whose stakes run into the thousands of dollars," Cobb acknowledges. By the same token, of course, there are some who follow real-life sports primarily for the sake of betting on them. So popular has rotisserie ball become that inmates at the federal prison camp in

Allenwood, Pennsylvania, have organized a league behind bars. Reflecting the fact that many at Allenwood are former lawyers, accountants, politicians, and others convicted of such white-collar crimes as fraud and embezzlement, their teams tend toward names like the Clippers or the Swindlers. The prison's His Honors team belongs to a former city mayor imprisoned for accepting illegal payoffs. Allenwood owners do not play with real cash, since any form of gambling is prohibited by institution rules. Their league is "just for fun," one convicted drug smuggler maintains virtuously.

Other rotisserie players would say the same of their game. Cobb calls it "the greatest game for baseball fans since baseball." But Paul Belinkie, writing in the *New York Times,* points to concerns about the effect the pretend game may be having on the real one. "The argument has been made," he says, "that rotisserie baseball has had a negative influence on fans because [rotisserie] owners lose rooting interest in teams that may have been their favorites since childhood." Indeed, Nathan Cobb traces his preoccupation with rotiss to the night in October 1986 when his childhood favorite Boston Red Sox blew the World Series they were just one putout away from winning over the New York Mets. "To this day," says the disaffected Cobb, "I do not care if the Red Sox win, lose or move to Dubuque."

If that "don't care" attitude toward real sports and its actual stars characterizes some rotisserie players, a similar distancing on the part of fans may be detected in the current craze for collecting sports memorabilia. It's one thing to trade Little League pins with members of other teams or to save and swap baseball cards. That sort of collecting is fun and a time-honored way for fans to build a sense of kinship with a game and its stars. But collecting is something else again when it's carried out on the scale of a Wayne Gretzky. Owning an eighty-year-old piece of cardboard that measures one-and-a-half inches by two-and-five-eighths inches and is so valuable that its logical home is in a bank vault isn't just fun. It's serious business.

The seriousness doesn't rule out the fact that Gretzky probably enjoys being part owner of a card of such unique sentimental value. But mustn't he and his partner also see the card as an investment that they hope will increase in value against the day they may want to sell it? And mustn't they sometimes wonder about the financial wisdom of tying up $410,000 in something that was worth only $25,000 five years before they bought it? Baseball card prices don't always rise. They may hold steady—or drop. The 1952 Mickey Mantle card that sold for $500 in 1981 and $10,000 a decade later was priced at $3,000 in 1979. From $3,000 in '79 down to $500 in '81 represents a loss of five-sixths of its value in two years. Surely, the pleasure of owning such a rarity must be tempered by thoughts of money. To the extent that it is, old-fashioned collecting takes a backseat to finance.

There are other indications that sports collecting as a business threatens to overwhelm the kind of collecting devoted fans once did strictly for fun. One was the 1991 announcement by managers at the Topps Company—the gum makers who pioneered the bubble-gum-baseball card combination—that they would no longer include gum with their trading cards. Why not? Because the sticky stuff sometimes stained the cards, decreasing their monetary value. Another was the 1990 creation of the National Collectors Exchange for baseball cards (NACEX). Computer-equipped to monitor the cards' fluctuating values electronically, NACEX prepared to introduce stock market methods to sports collecting. A third sign that collecting for fun may be giving way to collecting for profit is the new rancor surrounding sports autographs.

Autograph collecting used to be as uncomplicated a hobby as collecting baseball cards. Kids hung around the ballpark, hoping to intercept their favorite sports stars and get them to scrawl their names on a scoreboard or other souvenir. Team owners and managers kept stocks of balls in the clubhouse and nagged at players to sign them for promotional purposes. Such autographed keepsakes were regarded as purely personal treasures by those lucky enough to own one. "Now it's different," says sportswriter Dave Anderson. "Now autographs are big business." Their extraordinary dollars and cents value has done more than change the reason people want sports autographs. It's also changed the way people ask for them—and the spirit in which stars give them.

E. M. Swift described in *Sports Illustrated* the frantic autograph hunt that followed baseball's post–All Star Game party in 1990. It was 2:45 A.M., and Dave Parker of the Milwaukee Brewers was starting across a hotel lobby when "chaos" erupted. "'There's Parker!' says a high-pitched voice. A kid in a red baseball cap springs to his feet. . . . A dozen youngsters, some as young as 11 years old, pursue Parker up the escalator, pleading, cajoling, whining as they scramble to find his baseball card in the plastic-covered pages of their scrapbooks." One eleven-year-old tells Swift that he's been in the lobby over seven hours waiting for this moment. What will the young fan do with the signature now that he finally has it? "Sometimes we sell the stuff," the boy confides.

The entrepreneurial frenzy isn't limited to baseball—nor to kids. Golfer Seve Ballesteros reported having to "shoo away fans of all ages" on the fairways as he tried to practice for the 1990 British Open. Cincinnati Bengals passing leader Boomer Esiason, forced out of a first-class seat and into coach on a commercial airline, found the flight turned into a nightmarish four-hour-long signing session. "I couldn't go anywhere," he says. "I was trapped." Fellow NFLer Randall Cunningham of the Philadelphia Eagles has shared the trapped feeling. Cunningham also notices a change from the autograph seekers of the past: "It used to be just kids. Now it's guys 35 to 40 years old. They'll come at you with a stack of 40 cards and want you to sign them all." Anyone who's looking to get forty identical cards signed by the same star isn't collecting for the fun of it. That person is in business. "It's getting out of hand," complains the Philadelphia Flyers' Ron Hextall. Other players agree.

Fans, increasingly, do not. Sports stars are pulling in plenty, aren't they? So let them give a little something back in return—that's the average fan's attitude. Even harder for fans to stomach is the arrogance with which players may react to the pressure to sign. Some are openly irritable with autograph seekers, even polite ones. Others refuse to sign at all unless they are paid for doing so, and pay arrangements can be controversial. On one occasion, Chicago Cubs shortstop Shawon Dunston negotiated a $4,300 fee for an autographing session to benefit an Iowa public library. Then, four days before the scheduled event, Dunston declared that he would not appear unless his payment was upped to $5,500. The charity's organizers met the demand, but made no secret of their disgust at this show of petty greed on the part of a ballplayer earning $1.2 million a year.

The infusion of adult-sized stacks of money into what was once a kids' hobby is doing nothing to bring fans closer to sport and its players. In fact, it is having quite the opposite effect, alienating fans to a degree that some see as alarming. And now government is getting into the act. In 1991, state lawmakers in New York and Michigan were asked to consider enacting bills aimed at protecting the public from greedy or unscrupulous sports memorabilia dealing.

The Michigan proposal would make it a misdemeanor, punishable by a $500 fine, for any active athlete to accept money for signing autographs. The bill would exempt former stars from its provisions since, as its chief sponsor says, "they didn't make that much money when they were playing." The New York measure was to be aimed at protecting autograph buyers cheated into investing in forged signatures, something that happens more and more often in the newly profitable world of sports memorabilia. If passed, the legislation would require dealers who sell autographs for $50 or more to provide certificates of authenticity. Any dealer found to have authenticated a fake would have to return the defrauded buyer's money—times three. Dave Anderson applauds the idea of such a law, but adds that "there's no charm" in a business that requires it.

As some see it, the charm is fading throughout much of the sports world. Modern sport has come a long way from traditional game playing and even from its own eighteenth- and nineteenth-century roots. As sport becomes more and more of a business, it becomes less and less the casual leisure-time entertainment to which fans originally lent their support—and thereby helped to create. Now that creation is slipping out of the reach of ordinary fans. Or so some believe.

Certainly a trip to the ballpark or stadium is getting beyond the means of a great many fans. As the 1990 baseball season opened, *Sports Illustrated* compared the cost of going to a game that year with what it had cost in 1950. In 1950, *SI* found, the average price of a major-league ticket was $1.60. Average for 1990, $8. (The next year, ticket prices jumped another 9 percent, or 72¢, on average.) Since four decades of rising prices meant that 1950's $1.60 was equivalent to $8.23 in 1990, $8 or $9 tickets represented quite a bargain.

They were about the last bargain fans were likely to come

across. The hot dog that cost 10¢ in 1951 went for $2.50 forty years later, *SI* says. That's almost $2 more than the 51¢ it would have cost due to price increases based on inflation alone. For a family of four, $2.50 hot dogs mean an outlay of $10 just for food—assuming that no one is thirsty and everyone satisfied with one snack. Or with so plebeian a snack. Fancier—costlier—fare is to be had: pizza rolls, fried chicken, chef's salads, strawberry shortcake, Buffalo-style chicken wings, and, in some West Coast sports facilities, Japanese sushi. Transportation and parking costs have risen over the years, and so have the prices of such items as programs and the licensed goods that no one even dreamed of trying to sell back in the fifties. "It's not hard," says the Associated Press's Steve Wilstein, "for a family of four to spend $100 before heading home from the game." Not every U.S. family can afford $100 for an outing at the park.

Not everyone can afford to show up at other types of sporting events. The cheapest ticket to a game at New York's Madison Square Garden, home to the basketball Knicks and hockey Rangers, cost $16 in 1992. The best courtside seats at the Garden went from $35 in 1989 to $45 the next year to $65 the year after that. Top prices for Portland Trail Blazers games hit $150 in 1990. And these are the prices for everyday events. When an important contest is in the offing, ticket "scalpers" get into the act. Scalpers are speculators who buy up blocks of seats in advance and sell them at the last minute for whatever the market will bear. Scalpers' prices for a single seat at the 1992 Super Bowl ranged from $475 to $1,500. During a baseball championship play-off series, a scalper can get as much as $35 each for seats he picked up for $3.50 apiece. Scalpers' rates are the exception, and since their seats are in such demand they generally sell out. But with prices sky-high even for routine events, no one should be surprised if regular-season seats go unsold.

Going unsold was just what too many seats were beginning to do in the early 1990s. Once again in America, the economic times were tough, not as tough as during the Great Depression of the 1930s, but bad enough. People were losing their jobs—and their ability to spend on sports entertainment. Officials in both horse and auto racing reported declining fan support in 1990 and 1991. In team sports, the National Hockey League was particularly hard hit. According to NHL figures, 12.58 million fans attended games during the 1989–90 season. That number dipped to 12.34 million the next year, a drop of 2 percent. Although some teams, notably the Minnesota North Stars and the San Jose Sharks, enjoyed strong ticket sales, overall NHL attendance decreased by a further percentage point during the first month of the 1991–92 season. At pricey Madison Square Garden, the Rangers' attendance slipped even more precipitously, from an average 17,402 a game in 1984–85 to an average of 15,964 six years later, a decline of 8.3 percent. Despite their standing as Stanley Cup champions at the end of the 1990–91 season, the Pittsburgh Penguins reported selling 150 fewer seats per game after raising ticket prices by $5 the next year. In New Jersey, the Devils played in front of crowds of 10,000 or 11,000 in an arena built to hold 19,040. Uneasy league officials noted that the empty-seat phenomenon was more noticeable at the $16- or $20-a-seat level than at the $65 level. Fans well off enough to blow $65 on a hockey game were apparently unaffected by the economic downturn. Besides, expensive seats are often bought up by corporations and used for entertaining business clients, meaning that their cost can be written off as a tax deduction. Not so the seats bought by the regular working people who make up the bulk of any team's fans. For them, tickets are an out-of-pocket expense.

Was expense the only thing keeping hockey fans at home as the 1990s began? League owners hoped so. After all, bad times are generally followed by good, and if a lack of money was all that was standing between the sport and its fans, things would change as the economy improved. But what if money weren't the only problem?

There were signs that it might not be. It wasn't just at the arena that fans were giving NHL play the cold shoulder. Hockey is the only one of the country's four major professional team sports without a network television contract. Broadcast executives have hesitated to offer one, suspecting that games might not attract enough of an audience to allow them to charge advertisers top dollar for airtime. Instead, the NHL contracts with cable television. And the cable deal that NHL officials signed for their 1991–92 season was for $5.5 million, two-thirds *less* than what they got in each of the three previous years. On a brighter note, ABC-TV indicated that it might broadcast up to twelve NHL games in 1993. On a darker one, hockey games are likelier than games in other sports to be broadcast on a pay-per-view basis. Can hockey hang on to its following if fans must pay $10 or more to watch regular-season play in their own living rooms?

Similar questions crop up in other sports. The 1990 broadcast of the Holyfield-Douglas title fight, the one that cost $34.95 on pay cable, was cut short in the third round when the ill-prepared Douglas received a knockout blow. Are boxing fans going to go on indefinitely thinking it's worthwhile to spend so much to see a three-round mismatch? Even more thrilling contests may not attract paying television audiences. Along with its network coverage of the 1992 Summer Olympics, NBC offered a 15-day cable package at a cost to viewers of $125. Only 125,000 homes signed up at that price, and NBC admitted losing as much as $40 million on the deal. Will football fans accept pay-per-view as the wave of the future? Paul Tagliabue wants them to. Early in his tenure as

NFL commissioner, Tagliabue expressed the desire to begin experimenting with pay viewing by 1993. Sports agent Leigh Steinberg thought that was a bad idea. "Long-term, pay-per-view threatens the popularity of sports," he warned. "In the long run it will wipe out high percentages of younger fans, lower income fans . . . Because in a sport like football, it already is not accessible live (in person) to most fans." Not accessible, Steinberg meant, because ticket prices and related costs are becoming so exorbitant.

Even network sports broadcasting, the kind that comes "free" (in exchange for viewers' willingness to spend a good portion of their time absorbing advertising messages) has been losing fan support. Dismally low ratings halted the NFL's World League of American Football operations in 1992, although those in charge of the league promised a return in 1994. The NFL itself could be in trouble. "The average audience for *Monday Night Football* . . . has been declining for a decade," says Mark Landler of *Business Week* magazine. Landler and others point out that CBS-TV took a terrible beating on the four-year $1.06 billion deal it struck with major-league baseball to air games between 1990 and 1994. Viewership for the network's 1990 baseball league championships was down 12 percent from the previous year. Nineteen ninety-one was another bad year for CBS sports, although the size of that year's World Series audience came as a pleasant surprise. Still, even in the wake of the Series, Commissioner Vincent felt compelled to warn owners that shrinking numbers of viewers could mean one-third less revenue for the league when it came time to write the television contract for 1994. Cable sportscasting has had its troubles, too, with all-sports ESPN coming up more than 60 percent short on audience estimates for its Sunday-night baseball games in 1990.

Why the drop-off in fan interest? One possibility: too many hours of sports programming for too few viewers. Landler cites figures showing 7,300 network and cable hours of athletics in 1989 compared to 4,600 in 1980. But other forces may also be at work, more signs of genuine trouble between sport and its fans.

Because sport is in trouble with the fans. "You lousy, over-paid piece of ——!" sportswriter Nicholas Dawidoff reported hearing one Boston Red Sox fan yell at a player during a 1991 game at Fenway Park. "Sit down and ——." "So what are you —— complaining about, you ——?" another shouted in the next inning. The fans weren't screaming at the other team's players. They were addressing the home team, and their remarks were nothing unusual for the 1990s. Jose Canseco has had to endure taunts about his troubled marriage as well as put up with ethnic remarks. "Go back to Cuba!" one spectator—later ejected from the park—shrieked at the Havana-born outfielder. That's not good-natured razzing; it's vicious racism. Equally vicious was the sarcastic "invitation" extended by a fan to Albert Belle of the Cleveland Indians. "Keg party at my house after the game!" the fan shouted, honing in cruelly on Belle's history of alcoholism. Belle struck back at his tormentor—literally—hurling a ball directly at his chest from fifteen feet away. The man was injured, though not seriously, and Belle was suspended for a week. Discord between fans and athletes mars other sports. Defensive end Bruce Smith of the Buffalo Bills threatened to quit the team after its 1992 Super Bowl appearance. The reason he gave: an influx of racist hate mail excoriating him for failing to play following knee surgery. Spectators at hockey games have been known to plunge right into the action when fights break out on the ice. Tennis fans, who once limited themselves to hushed murmurs and subdued clapping, loudly boo and jeer.

Why the breakdown in civility? "Part of it is when you pay your $8 you give yourself permission to yell," suggests Jerry M. Lewis, sociology professor at Kent State University in Ohio. Or your $16 or $65. Or your $150. Another part may have to do with the athletes' exposure in the media. Babe Ruth drank to excess and indulged in extramarital affairs, but since the public didn't know about his problems, no one baited him by mentioning keg parties or girlfriends. Still another part could be the result of the stars' own game-time behavior. Tennis fans used to seeing an Andre Agassi smashing racquets or a John McEnroe hurling insults at the linesmen may feel inclined to react with some verbal violence of their own. But the biggest reason for fan discourtesy is linked, many believe, to modern sports salaries.

"Fans are less and less able to identify with obscenely overpaid athletes," comments writer John Underwood. The lack of identification may help explain why fans turn even on players they would once have revered as hometown heroes. "Can someone who is being paid a million dollars a year . . . to throw a ball in a basket be tolerated when he misses the basket?" Underwood asks. Apparently not.

Wilbert McClure, a Boston psychologist and boxing gold medalist in the 1960 Olympics, agrees that high salaries contribute to a growing division between sport stars and their fans—and points out that the division is felt on both sides. When he was an active athlete, McClure remembers, "There was more of an equality between the athlete and the fan. Guys starting [in sports] now are thinking bucks and fame. The fan is someone who is like an afterthought . . . [Sport is] really a business, and that gives [athletes] a different perspective of their relationship with fans." Gives athletes a different perspective on sport itself, too. "They are making awesome amounts of money for a really short period of time," McClure says, "and so they are under a lot of stress. It makes it difficult for guys today to see it as a game."

Perhaps it's also difficult for fans to pick out the playful elements in the business that modern sport has become. Sport today is drenched in commercialism. Look around the playing field. It appears to belong, not to the team, not to the city that may have paid for building it, but to Volvo, Miller Lite, American Express, and a dozen other companies. Listen to the announcements about which sponsor owns this inning, this quarter, this set, and is gracious enough to be "bringing it to you." Watch the players, metamorphosed by endorsement deals into living, breathing, sweating billboards promoting Nikes, Converse, Gatorade, and Pepsi. Of course fans feel alienated. Follow the plays: the pass that earns the distinction of being the Canon Camcorder Play of the Day, the punt return that wins the Avis We Try Harder Award, the Budweiser Dunk of the Game. Even the plays don't belong to the players who make them. They're corporate property. Catch up on the action (you may have missed a play during a commercial break) courtesy of the Marine Corps Scoreboard, the Fruit of the Loom Halftime Report, the *New York Times*'s Pat Riley Post-Game Press Conference, or the Head and Shoulders NFL Live Postgame Report. Tune in, if you can stand all the bad news, for the United States Healthcare Injury Report. "The U.S. has demonstrated its ability to drown a sport in . . . sponsorships and endorsements," says George Black of *The Nation*. At that, references to Budweiser Dunks and Head and Shoulders wrap-ups don't count as ads. They've become part of the action.

Other factors help place barriers between fans and the games they love. Once, fans were a part of sport, so deeply a part that they helped direct the way it grew and changed. In England, men, women, and children watched delighted as medieval football turned into two distinctly different games, soccer, which emphasizes kicking, and rugby, a running, tackling game. American fans and players preferred a running-kicking-tackling combination of both. Crowds applauded wildly as the game grew faster and rougher, their enthusiasm encouraging so much violence that in 1906 the rules were changed to protect players. One change permitted players to advance the ball by throwing it, and that's how the forward pass came to be. At first, teams resisted using the new play, but by the 1920s its popularity among fans—passing added to the game's excitement—had made it standard.

Today, changes in the way games are played seem to come about for reasons that have little if anything to do with what fans want to see. We've already noted how the financial demands of television, especially, are leading leagues and associations to modify their rules, adding designated hitters here, subtracting minutes from a halftime break there, altering scoring methods, and adopting tiebreakers. Some of the innovations, tiebreakers, for instance, add to a game's excitement, but many are profit-driven nuisances. Football players say that shortened breaks don't allow them enough of a rest and fans probably aren't crazy about seeing the game hurried along, but the NFL is unlikely to disappoint network executives by returning to its old rules. If, on the other hand, baseball's American League acts on suggestions that it drop its designated hitter rule and go back to having pitchers take their turns at bat, that, too, will be for a business reason. Team owners want to save the cost of paying high salaries to sluggers who contribute nothing to defense. How *fans* feel about designated hitters is not likely to have much to do with anything.

We've also seen how business considerations disrupt teams themselves, further alienating fans. Some players concentrate more on improving their personal playing statistics—impressive stats mean an impressive paycheck—than on helping the team. Free agents rove restlessly from club to club, league to league, nation to nation, coolly abandoning fellow players and fans alike in search of the best deal. Worse, the emphasis on profit has whole teams on the move. The franchise shifts that began in 1953 with the Boston Braves' flight to Milwaukee estranged one generation of fans. Now, a threatened new series of moves may do the same to another.

Several franchise shifts were under consideration in the 1990s. New England football fans spent much of 1992 assessing rumors about possible moves by the Patriots. As the 1992 baseball season drew to a close, the San Francisco Giants announced a move—promptly vetoed by baseball owners—to St. Petersburg, Florida. Another baseball club, the Seattle Mariners, had its first-ever winning season in 1991, and Seattle fans rewarded the team by breaking all home attendance records. Their enthusiasm may have been misplaced: only weeks later, Mariners owner Jeff Smulyan was talking about deserting Seattle for some other city.

Can fans do anything to protect a team they've come to love? They sure can—buy its loyalty. Smulyan set his price for staying in Seattle at $10 million a year. A millionaire broadcasting executive from Indianapolis, Smulyan claimed that record attendance or not, the Mariners were losing money. Gate receipts alone were not enough to allow him to turn a profit, he told the citizens of Seattle. If they wanted the team to stay put, they could tap their municipal treasury and help him foot his bills.

Jeff Smulyan is far from being the only sports investor who has tried to force local fans to pick up the tab for keeping a team in town. Football's Al Davis, owner of the Los Angeles Raiders, put the screws on that city in 1990, dangling before its fans the possibility that he would shift his franchise back to Oakland, from which it had moved nine years before. To get Davis to stay with them, Los Angeles promoters agreed to several concessions, including paying him $20 million in two installments and spending $150 million more to renovate Memorial Stadium, the team's home. Oakland city leaders, hoping to lure the Raiders back to their territory, countered by offering to guarantee Davis $602 million in ticket sales over fifteen years. The guarantee meant that if fans bought anything less than $602 million worth of seats in that time, the city would make up the difference.

Once, the struggle between Oakland and L.A. might have been long and bitter, with fans in each city willing to make almost any financial sacrifice for the sake of claiming the team as their own. Back thirty years ago, for instance, San Francisco put $15 million into building Candlestick Park for the city's newly acquired Giants. In the early seventies, the people of Philadelphia sunk $38 million into Veterans Stadium, now home to the Phillies and the Eagles. Early in the 1990s, St. Petersburg unveiled a new, $139 million, domed stadium constructed with public money in anticipation of winning one of the new National League baseball franchises. St. Petersburg fans were disappointed, though; the Florida franchise was awarded to Fort Lauderdale.

For their part, the people of Oakland had no intention of digging themselves into a financial hole in the hope of acquiring a sports franchise. Guarantee the Raiders $602 million over fifteen years? At a time when crime and illegal drugs were flooding city streets and the public schools were desperate for cash? In a 1990 election, Oakland voters turned on the mayor who had supported the guarantee proposal, dumping him from office. Two years later, people in San Jose displayed similar coolness toward their mayor's suggestion that taxes be increased to finance a $185 million stadium to attract a new professional franchise. Seattle never did raise the $10 million a year required to keep the Mariners in town; instead, the team was sold to a group of private investors.

Why the reluctance to put up public money to attract or retain a sports organization? Much of it had to do with the floundering economy of the 1990s. The people of Oakland had made that plain. But what if the foot-dragging sprang from something more besides? What if it was one more symptom of that new sense of alienation and resentment among sports fans?

If it was, perhaps sport has only itself to blame. It's sport, after all, that is demonstrating to fans that what counts most is money. It's sport that sets the example, choosing big salaries over loyalty to a club or a city, putting corporate well-being ahead of the well-being of a team and its players, embracing profits, not fans.

Yet it is to the fans that sport belongs. Without them, what future can it have?

Chapter 8

Sport in a New Century

What lies ahead for sport? The question was on the minds of a great many people as the twentieth century began drawing to a close.

Thoughts of the future had baseball commissioner Fay Vincent worried as early as 1991. "Baseball is poised for a catastrophe," he told reporters that year. "And it might not be far off." To Vincent, the chief problem was the spiraling player salaries that threatened to bankrupt all but the richest of clubs. Perhaps owners should institute salary caps as a means of dealing with the situation, Vincent suggested. Or they might adopt profit-sharing programs to keep club salaries in line with club incomes. But they must do something, and soon, he warned, or some franchises could go under financially. Baseball owners were worried about money, too, but instead of following Vincent's advice, they turned on him, voting to demand that he resign as commissioner. In September 1992, Vincent did just that.

Steeply rising salaries were worrying the NFL's Paul Tagliabue, too, particularly in light of the 1992 court case that limited owners' ability to curb wages through their Plan B free agent system. An end to Plan B almost certainly meant the start of a new round of wage hikes, and that prospect was enough to make the league drop the two-team expansion previously scheduled for 1994. In addition, Tagliabue was urging team owners to impose wage restrictions on rookie players and, possibly, to adopt salary caps for all players at the same time. Professional hockey owners also had serious salary concerns. Only in the NBA, where salary caps had been in place for years, were minds relatively at ease—on this issue, at least.

For salaries were just one worrisome subject in the sports world. The NHL had declining ticket sales and a complete lack of network television exposure to ponder as well. Fay Vincent had reminded baseball owners that after 1994, when their $1.06 billion CBS-TV contract expired, they could expect to see a sharp drop in their television revenues. On the college sports level, one longtime worry materialized at the end of 1991: the Internal Revenue Service began knocking at the door. In December, the IRS ruled for the first time that the business sponsors of college bowl games could not claim the money spent as a tax deduction. Corporate sports sponsorship is not a charity, the IRS said, but a form of advertising and, as such, taxable. Colleges greeted the news with dismay. If even a few companies gave up their sponsorships, as seemed possible, some bowl games might be wiped out. Professional golf had sponsorship problems, too. In 1991, four major backers closed their checkbooks to the PGA tour. "The golden goose is dead," one sports advertising executive commented. According to him, PGA commissioner Deane Beman had only himself to blame for the sponsor loss. "Greed got the better part of him," the executive said of Beman. In his view, pro golf had "cannibalized" itself by overscheduling events.

Sports sponsorship was also a worry at network television headquarters. Viewerships for sports events were down, and advertisers were digging in their heels and insisting upon bargain rates for airtime. Advertising minutes during CBS-TV's

1992 Super Bowl game and Winter Olympics did not sell out until hours before the broadcasts were set to begin. The network lost $55 million on its 1990 major-league baseball schedule. The next year, CBS reported total losses of $400 million—most of that attributable to its mammoth sports splurge. Executives at cable television systems that offer pay-per-view sportscasting were also experiencing disappointment. Of the twenty million homes equipped to receive pay cable, only a couple of million were buying the systems' best sports sellers, their heavily advertising boxing matches.

Other problems were worrying the sports world. There were long-standing concerns like drug abuse, gambling, and racial and sexual discrimination. College sport had its recurring recruitment scandals and won't-go-away violations of NCAA rules regarding the athletic, academic, and financial treatment of players. The NCAA itself was the target of unprecedented levels of criticism. And there was a terrible new problem. Magic Johnson's 1991 AIDS announcement had been a shocker that raised some deeply disturbing questions. Might other players be infected? If so, was it possible for them to spread the deadly virus—through bleeding from cuts, for example? Should athletes be tested routinely for the virus that causes AIDS? Infected players be allowed to compete? Johnson, although retired from regular play, did show up for the NBA's 1992 All-Star contest. He scored twenty-five points and won the game's Most Valuable Player award. A few months later, Johnson traveled to the Summer Olympics as part of the gold-medal American "Dream Team." But his plans to return to the pro court in time for the 1992–93 season fell through when several players went public with their concerns about competing against someone with the AIDS-causing virus.

Some sports had their own special worries for the 1990s. Boxing's future looked troubled, what with the sport's dependence upon faltering pay cable sales and the bad publicity that resulted from the Mike Tyson rape conviction. Tennis was hearing more and more criticism about the way it treats young players, admitting them into professional tournaments in their early teens, only to have too many of them give up the game just as they were at the point of reaching their full playing strength. As a fourteen-year-old in 1990, Jennifer Capriati got off to a stunning start, but two years later she was in tears after caving in to pressure and losing the quarterfinals at the Australian Open. Pete Sampras, nineteen when he won $2 million in the 1990 Grand Slam Cup tournament, "limped, cringed and complained" his way through 1991, according to *New York Times* reporter Robin Finn. Angelica Gavaldon, who turned pro at age sixteen, quit the game after her seventeenth birthday in 1991. "I couldn't face one more hotel, one more airport or another tennis club," she told reporters.

No wonder the sports world is worried. Burned-out players, new problems like AIDS and old ones like drugs, shaky attendance figures, reluctant sponsors, soaring salaries . . . it's a prescription for trouble. And that's just the beginning. Sports agent Leigh Steinberg sees a bigger trouble ahead, one that may be a consequence of sport's other problems. Sport, Steinberg says, may be losing its "fantasy element."

What is that element? Sport as it lives in the imagination: sport with its hopes and dreams, its happy endings, its stubborn courage in the face of great odds. It is sport's fantasy element that casts its mystic aura upon young worshipers at the ancient Olympics, that honors Abner Doubleday as the inventor of baseball, that enshrines as heroes those ordinary people who chance to have extraordinary athletic talent. It's the fantasy element that turned the 1992 World Series into a modern-day fairy tale, that makes a true fan cherish even the stickiest of baseball cards, that creates the national obsession we call Super Bowl Sunday. Sport's fantasy element is what makes sport great, and preserving that element is, in Steinberg's opinion, essential. "We're going to have to watch very carefully that [it] not be destroyed," he warns. "Because to the extent that the sports page reads like the business section, or even worse the crime beat section, then fans will lose their fascination for sports."

Some people say they're already losing it. "I think spectator sports are going away," John Naisbitt said in 1991. Naisbitt is a futurist, someone who measures trends—social, economic, political, religious—and predicts how those trends may grow and change in years to come. One trend Naisbitt sees these days is Americans turning away from the kind of sporting events in which they have delighted since the days of the Industrial Revolution.

As Naisbitt sees things, modern consumer sport, which rose with the start of a new industrial age, may decline with it. Like Allen Guttmann and Richard Mandell, Naisbitt sees parallels between life in the factory and life on the playing field, between the precise, fast-moving production line and precise, fast-moving sports contests. Now, though, our industrialized society is changing into a technological and informational one. That change, Naisbitt believes, is bound to be reflected in changes in Americans' leisure-time tastes. As evidence, he points to the fact that in the 1970s, Americans spent twice as much on tickets to sporting events as they did on tickets for such arts entertainment as plays, museums, and concerts. During the 1980s, the arts began catching up. "Sports are being replaced by the fine arts as the dominant leisure activity of the society," he concludes.

Leigh Steinberg disagrees, prophesying a whole different future for sports. "I believe we'll see the emergence of new sports," he says. They'll be "sports built for television" with "tremendous action" modeled on that of video games. "TV-ready sports will have every aspect of them worked out up front," Steinberg continues, "from ownership of the franchises to merchandising rights. The rules will be simple enough to follow and there will be a high degree of violence and action to them." Steinberg sounds as if he could have been describing television's "American Gladiators." Does that show represent the way of the future for sports?

Allen Guttmann doesn't think so. In his view, our spectator sports aren't likely to change much in the twenty-first century. There'll just be more of them. "It is likely that the leagues will continue to expand and be joined by new leagues in new sports with new television contracts," Guttmann says. Soccer, for example, may be about to make it big in the United States. Sport is likely to become increasingly specialized, with baseball perhaps adopting football's platoon system and becoming a game with separate teams for fielding and batting. Numbers and statistics may assume even greater significance, thanks to advancing computer technology.

Whatever happens, though, our passion for sport will not die. Participatory sports are growing in popularity, with jogging, skiing, fishing, playing tennis and golf—activities on which we Americans already spend $125 billion a year, $70 billion more than we spend on consumer sports—more and more our sports of choice. But consumer sports won't disappear. Some games may stagnate, dragged down by greed and corruption until they are little more than lifeless money machines. Yet others will survive and adapt and new ones will take the place of those that fail. For sports are a celebration of human achievement—and that is a celebration that can never end.

Bibliography

Chapter 1

Allen, Kevin. "Stevens' Deal Could Set Expensive Precedent." *USA Today,* July 12, 1990.

Associated Press. "Canseco Rips Clark." *Kennebec Journal,* July 6, 1990.

"A Whole New Ball Game." Research by Richard Sandomir, James Rodewald, and STATS, Inc. *Sports Illustrated,* April 16, 1990.

Berkow, Ira. "Better Than This There Never Was." *The New York Times,* October 29, 1991.

Brown, Clifton. "Ewing Becomes Richest; Bonilla Is on Deck." *The New York Times,* November 23, 1991.

Carlson, Timothy. "Pitching, Dribbling and Tackling for Megabucks." *TV Guide,* August 11, 1990.

Chass, Murray. "Series Is Over, but the Relish Remains." *The New York Times,* October 29, 1991.

Diaz, Jaime. "Season on the Links: More Prosperity Is Just Around the Next Dogleg." *The New York Times,* January 6, 1992.

Finn, Robin. "New Season Will Probably Be a Spinoff of '91." *The New York Times,* January 13, 1992.

———. "Seles Stuns Graf to Capture French Open Title." *The New York Times,* June 10, 1990.

———. "U.S. Open Looking for a New TV Contract, Too." *The New York Times,* July 27, 1990.

Gammon, Clive. "The Long Goodbye." *Sports Illustrated,* February 2, 1990.

Henry, William A., III. "Stalking Memories at Wimbledon." *Time,* July 2, 1990.

Johnson, William Oscar. "The Cleanup Hitters." *Sports Illustrated,* June 28, 1990.

Koppett, Leonard. "Canseco Becomes $5 Million Man." *The New York Times,* June 28, 1990.

Lieberman, David. "Anatomy of a Deal." *TV Guide,* August 11, 1990.

Litsky, Frank. "Taylor Seeks a Raise to $2 Million." *The New York Times,* May 23, 1990.

———. "Taylor and Marshall Lead List of 13 Missing Giants." *The New York Times,* July 24, 1990.

Looney, Douglas S. "Rapid Bobbin'." *Sports Illustrated,* July 23, 1990.

Newcomb, Peter, and Palmeri, Christopher. "Throw a Tantrum, Sign a Contract." *Forbes,* August 20, 1990.

Smith, Claire. "Fitting Ending for a Storybook Series." *The New York Times,* October 29, 1991.

Solloway, Steve. "Grand National Drivers Pursue Pot of Gold." *Maine Sunday Telegram,* July 8, 1990.

Thigpen, David E. "Real-Life Days of Thunder." *Time,* July 30, 1990.

Chapter 2

Cavanaugh, Jack. "Hartford Paper First Up to Bat." *The New York Times,* August 9, 1990.

Guttmann, Allen. *A Whole New Ball Game.* Chapel Hill and London: University of North Carolina Press, 1988.

———. *From Ritual to Record: The Nature of Modern Sports.* New York: Columbia University Press, 1978.

Janofsky, Michael. "29-4 1/2! Soaring Powell Conquers Beamon's Record." *The New York Times,* August 31, 1991.

Koppett, Leonard. *Sports Illusion, Sports Reality.* Boston: Houghton Mifflin, 1981.

Mandell, Richard. *Sport: A Cultural History.* New York: Columbia University Press, 1984.

McIntosh, Peter. *Fair Play: Ethics in Sport and Education.* London: Heinemann, 1979.

Newman, Gerald, ed. *The Concise Encyclopedia of Sports.* 2nd rev. ed. New York: Franklin Watts, 1979.

Chapter 3

Anderson, Dave. "And Now: N.L.'s Lost Weekend." *The New York Times,* October 6, 1990.

"A Signal Event." *Sports Illustrated,* Special Issue, Fall 1991.

Associated Press. "Notre Dame in Europe TV Deal." *The New York Times,* August 28, 1990.

———. "On Further Review, Instant Replay Dies." *The New York Times,* March 19, 1992.

———. "Stabler Criticizes NFL." *Kennebec Journal,* December 8, 1990.

Davidson, Gary, with Bill Libby. *Breaking the Game Wide Open.* New York: Atheneum, 1974.

Durso, Joseph. *The All-American Dollar: The Big Business of Sports.* Boston: Houghton Mifflin, 1971.

George, Thomas. "Under-3-Hour N.F.L. Game? New Rules Make It Possible." *The New York Times,* August 24, 1990.

Guttmann, Allen. *A Whole New Ball Game.* Chapel Hill and London: University of North Carolina Press, 1988.

Helyar, John. "Lure of TV Loot Loosens Old College Ties." *The Wall Street Journal,* November 14, 1990.

Johnson, William Oscar. "The Cleanup Hitters." *Sports Illustrated,* June 28, 1990.

Kelleher, Robert J. "Who Should Control Professional Tennis?" *The New York Times,* June 24, 1990.

Kelly, Kevin. "Let's Win One for the Coffers." *Business Week,* September 23, 1991.

Lapointe, Joe. "Familiar Sort of Scrutiny for New TV Deal." *The New York Times,* August 22, 1990.

Lineberry, William P., ed. *The Business of Sports.* New York: H. W. Wilson Company, 1973.

Mandell, Richard. *Sport: A Cultural History.* New York: Columbia University Press, 1984.

Newcomb, Peter, and Christopher Palmeri. "Throw a Tantrum, Sign a Contract." *Forbes,* August 20, 1990.

Noll, Roger G., ed. *Government and the Sports Business.* Washington, D.C.: The Brookings Institution, 1974.

Reed, William F. "We're Notre Dame and You're Not." *Sports Illustrated,* February 19, 1990.

Rhoden, William C. "Basketball Talent Search Brings Schoolboys to U.S." *The New York Times,* May 28, 1990.

Rosenthal, Phil. "NBC's $401M Olympic Gamble." *Kennebec Journal,* January 20, 1992.

Sandomir, Richard. "Networks Paying Less." *Kennebec Journal,* April 22, 1992.

Smart, Tim. "This May Be the Kick American Soccer Needs." *Business Week,* September 16, 1991.

Sperber, Murray. *College Sports, Inc.,* New York: Henry Holt, 1990.

Szilasi, Alix. "Tennis on TV: Too Much Talk." *The New York Times,* (letter), July 1, 1990.

Underwood, John. "Time for Colleges to Take Back the Field." *The New York Times,* July 22, 1990.

Yannis, Alex. "Sticking to Rules." *The New York Times,* August 19, 1990.

Chapter 4

Anderson, Dave. "Straw's $20 Million Burden." *The New York Times,* November 9, 1990.

Araton, Harvey. "Advertisers Shying from Magic's Touch." *The New York Times,* January 1, 1992.

Associated Press. "Bo Jackson Flunks His Football Physical." *The New York Times,* November 11, 1991.

———. "Doctor for Reds Quits." *The New York Times,* December 4, 1991.

———. "Jimmy Pushes Converse but He's Wearing Nikes." *Kennebec Journal,* September 7, 1991.

———. "NHL Owners Bought Time." *Kennebec Journal,* April 13, 1992.

———. "Pact for Bourque," *Kennebec Journal,* September 9, 1990.

Barrett, Todd. "Not Just Kid Stuff Anymore." *Newsweek,* October 30, 1990.

Berkow, Ira. "The Savage Pleasures of Football." *The New York Times,* November 26, 1991.

Brennan, Christine. "Sporting Life Weaves Warm Cocoon." *The Washington Post,* December 28, 1990.

Chass, Murray. "Citing Injury, Royals Decide to Release Jackson." *The New York Times,* March 19, 1991.

———. "Deal Reported on Settlement Payments in Collusion Case." *The New York Times,* December 7, 1990.

———. "Money, Money and More Money." *The New York Times,* November 21, 1991.

———. "Payroll Expansion: Ever-Widening Girth." *The New York Times,* December 16, 1990.

Douglas, Carlyle C. "The Pay for Hits, All Kinds, Goes Up." *The New York Times,* November 25, 1990.

Eskenazi, Gerald. "Toronto Lands N.F.L. Prospect in Rare Deal." *The New York Times,* April 22, 1991.

Finn, Robin. "Seles Fined $6,000 for Pulling Out of Wimbledon." *The New York Times,* June 25, 1991.

Foltz, Kim. "Does Bo, Hurt, Know as Much?" *The New York Times,* March 20, 1991.

Frey, Jennifer. "The Questions Are Lingering for Canseco." *The New York Times,* September 5, 1992.

George, Thomas. "N.F.L.'s Free-Agency System Is Found Unfair by U.S. Jury." *The New York Times,* September 11, 1992.

———. "Rash of Injuries Fires Up Debate," *The New York Times,* November 26, 1991.

Greenberg, Jay. "Scorecard." *Sports Illustrated,* September 16, 1991.

Guttmann, Allen. *A Whole New Ball Game.* Chapel Hill and London: University of North Carolina Press, 1988.

Helyar, John. "How Peter Ueberroth Led the Major Leagues in the 'Collusion Era.'" *The Wall Street Journal,* May 20, 1991.

Kelleher, Robert J. "Who Should Control Professional Tennis?" *The New York Times,* June 24, 1990.

King, Peter. "Risky Business." *Sports Illustrated,* September 10, 1990.

Kinney, Brendan. "The Scars of Playing the Game." *The New York Times,* August 26, 1990.

Kurkjian, Tim. "What Price Success?" *Sports Illustrated,* December 17, 1990.

Lapointe, Joe. "Macho? Yes. Violent? Without a Doubt. Hockey? Of Course." *The New York Times,* September 13, 1990.

McCallum, Jack. "And Many Happy Returns." *Sports Illustrated,* November 5, 1990.

Martinez, Michael. "The Sad and Abiding Legacy of Auto Racing." *The New York Times,* December 17, 1990.

Morganthau, Tom. "Sullivan: Bush's Aide Makes Waves." *Newsweek,* March 5, 1990.

Neff, Craig, and Lieber, Jill. "Behind the Scenes with George and Fay." *Sports Illustrated,* August 13, 1990.

Newcomb, Peter, and Palmeri, Christopher. "Throw a Tantrum, Sign a Contract." *Forbes,* August 20, 1990.

New York Times News Service. "Umps Sign Contract but Miss Openers." *Kennebec Journal,* April 9, 1991.

Noden, Merrell, ed. "Scorecard." *Sports Illustrated,* December 24, 1990.

Passell, Peter. "Those Big Executive Salaries May Mask a Bigger Problem." *The New York Times,* April 20, 1992.

Reif, Rita. "Honus Wagner Baseball Card Goes to Gretzky." *The New York Times,* March 23, 1991.

Rifkin, Glenn. "High Tops: High Style, High Tech, High Cost." *The New York Times,* January 5, 1992.

Sandomir, Richard. "Sports Officials Shrug Off Call for Smokeless Sponsors." *The New York Times,* April 12, 1991.

Smothers, Ronald. "Beer Opponents Start Their Engines." *The New York Times,* May 29, 1990.

Telander, Rick. "Senseless." *Sports Illustrated,* May 14, 1990.

Thigpen, David E. "Doing Well by Doing Good." *Time,* September 30, 1991.

Thomas, Robert McG., Jr. "Aching in Australia." *The New York Times,* January 13, 1991.

Vecsey, George. "What About the Other $386 Million?" *The New York Times,* January 17, 1992.

Wallace, William N. "In NFL, Many Are Freed but Few Find Jobs." *The New York Times,* January 31, 1991.

Weisman, Jacob. "Acolytes in the Temple of Nike." *The Nation,* June 17, 1991.

Wolff, Alexander. "High School Confidential." *Sports Illustrated,* January 8, 1990.

Wulf, Steve. "Scorecard." *Sports Illustrated,* October 21, 1991.

Yang, Dori Jones. "Step by Step with Nike." *Business Week,* August 13, 1990.

Chapter 5

"Alan Wiggins, Baseball Player, 32." *The New York Times,* obituary, January 9, 1991.

Alzado, Lyle, as told to Shelley Smith. "I'm Sick and I'm Scared." *Sports Illustrated,* July 8, 1991.

Associated Press. "Accused." *Kennebec Journal,* October 5, 1990.

——. "Avoided." *Kennebec Journal,* September 12, 1990.

——. "Charged." *Kennebec Journal,* October 5, 1990.

——. "Federal Study Cites Steroid Use by Teen-Agers." *The New York Times,* September 8, 1990.

——. "Fuhr Reinstated by NHL." *The New York Times,* February 5, 1991.

——. "Fuhr Used Cocaine, Paper Says." *The New York Times,* September 1, 1990.

——. "Leonard Tells of Drug Use." *The New York Times,* March 31, 1991.

——. "Maryland Coach Fined." *The New York Times,* September 13, 1990.

——. "Racism Outrages Williams in New Book, 'Quarterback.'" *Kennebec Journal,* August 30, 1990.

——. "Sentenced." *Kennebec Journal,* October 5, 1990.

——. "Smith Pleads Innocent to Vehicular Homicide." *Kennebec Journal,* March 23, 1991.

——. "Suspended." *Kennebec Journal,* August 7, 1990.

——. "Valvano Hired by ABC." *Kennebec Journal,* June 5, 1990.

Baker, Russell. "Boys Will Be Forever." *The New York Times,* October 2, 1990.

Berkow, Ira. "Bob Knight Recalls Len Bias." *The New York Times,* August 20, 1990.

Chass, Murray. "Board Says Rose Is Ineligible for Hall of Fame." *The New York Times,* February 5, 1991.

———. "Words, Inaction and Silence." *The New York Times,* September 14, 1991.

———. "Yanks Profess Concern for Howe Far Too Late." *The New York Times,* July 2, 1992.

Church, George J. "Why Pick on Pete?" *Time,* July 10, 1989.

Connolly, Pat. "It's Time to Ban Punitive Drug Testing." *The New York Times,* October 28, 1990.

Curry, Jack. "Arbitrator Puts Howe Back in Major Leagues." *The New York Times,* November 13, 1992.

Davidson, Miriam. "No King Holiday, Arizona Is Scorned." *The Christian Science Monitor,* December 3, 1990.

Eskenazi, Gerald. "Athletic Aggression and Sexual Assault." *The New York Times,* June 3, 1990.

———. "Leagues Faulted on Alcohol Policies." *The New York Times,* May 8, 1991.

Finch, Peter. "Racism: Golf's Intolerable Handicap." *Business Week,* August 13, 1990.

Fisher, Lawrence M. "Stamina-Building Drug Linked to Athletes' Deaths." *The New York Times,* May 19, 1991.

Gavin, M. F. Chip, "Winslow Hockey Players Suspended for Drugs." *Kennebec Journal,* January 30, 1992.

Gup, Ted. "Running Again—on Empty." *Time,* January 21, 1991.

Guttmann, Allen. *A Whole New Ball Game.* Chapel Hill and London: University of North Carolina Press, 1988.

Hoffer, Richard. "Howe and Why." *Sports Illustrated,* December 30, 1991.

Janofsky, Michael. "Athletes Who Cheat Face Tougher Testing." *The New York Times,* November 5, 1991.

———. "Drug Use by Prominent Athletes Reported." *The New York Times,* November 29, 1990.

———. "For Speed Skater, Competing Was Easy Part." *The New York Times,* December 24, 1991.

———. "Steinbrenner Returns to U.S. Olympic Post." *The New York Times,* January 21, 1991.

———. "2 U.S. Track Stars Face 2-Year Ban for Drug Use." *The New York Times,* November 6, 1990.

———. "U.S.O.C. Is Cashing in 5 Rings to State Lotteries." *The New York Times,* October 3, 1991.

Janovy, Jena. "The Spandex League." *The New York Times,* March 6, 1991.

Johnson, William Oscar. "A Sure Bet to Lower Debt." *Sports Illustrated,* September 2, 1991.

Katz, Bennett. "Red Sox Policies Should Open Up to All, of Every Race." *Kennebec Journal,* April 24, 1991.

Lipsyte, Robert. "What's Baseball Without a Beer?" *The New York Times,* October 25, 1991.

Litsky, Frank. "A Sportswriter's Place Is in the Locker Room." *The New York Times,* October 6, 1990.

McIntosh, Peter. *Fair Play: Ethics in Sport and Education.* London: Heinemann, 1979.

Mandell, Richard. *Sport: A Cultural History.* New York: Columbia University Press, 1984.

Moran, Malcolm, "Title IX Is Now an Irresistible Force." *The New York Times,* June 21, 1992.

Neff, Craig, and Lieber, Jill. "Bad Job, Baseball." *Sports Illustrated,* October 8, 1990.

Privman, Jay. "Valenzuela Back on Top of Things." *The New York Times,* April 28, 1992.

Quindlen, Anna. "No Problem." *The New York Times,* October 2, 1991.

———."The Cement Floor." *The New York Times,* August 28, 1991.

Reed, William F. "A Losing Bet." *Sports Illustrated,* August 26, 1991.

Rhoden, William C. "A Sudden Tinge of Conscience." *The New York Times,* September 13, 1991.

———. "Survival of the Fittest." *The New York Times,* November 1, 1991.

Rosenthal, Elisabeth, "Alzado Tumor Is Rare and Deadly." *The New York Times,* July 4, 1991.

Sandomir, Richard. "NBC Ratings Game Includes Bayou Classic." *The New York Times,* November 29, 1991.

Smith, Claire. "A Horror That Transcends Sport: Drinking and Driving." *The New York Times,* May 8, 1991.

———. "Baseball Failing in Minority Hiring, Officials Say." *The New York Times,* September 28, 1991.

———. "Belated Tribute to Baseball's Negro Leagues." *The New York Times,* August 13, 1991.

———. "Rose Sentenced to 5 Months for Filing False Tax Returns." *The New York Times,* July 20, 1990.

Smith, Timothy W. "Wyche Still Fighting on Locker Rooms." *The New York Times,* March 17, 1991.

Sperber, Murray. *College Sports, Inc.* New York: Henry Holt, 1990.

Stanley, Alessandra. "Among Baseball's Ball Girls, Fielding Skills Take 2nd Place." *The New York Times,* July 5, 1991.

Stevenson, Samantha. "Valenzuela Awaits the Verdict of His Peers." *The New York Times,* December 6, 1990.

Thomas, Robert McG., Jr. "Wyche Fined by NFL for Barring Female Writer." *The New York Times,* October 6, 1991.

Vecsey, George, "Gambling on Athletes Is Not Allowed Here," *The New York Times,* June 19, 1992.

———. "Arthur Ashe Confronts Apocalypse." *The New York Times,* June 8, 1991.

———. "Some Women Could Coach Men's Hoops." *The New York Times,* February 13, 1991.

———. "The League Serves Notice." *The New York Times,* November 28, 1990.

Wallace, William N. "Hofstra Quarterback Admits Use of Steroid." *The New York Times,* December 4, 1990.

Warner, Rick. "Mendes Remark Angered Rocket." *Kennebec Journal,* April 23, 1991.

Weiss, Ann E. *Lotteries: Who Wins, Who Loses?* Hillside, N.J.: Enslow Publishers, 1991.

Whitaker, Leslie. "Trouble in the Locker Rooms." *Time,* October 15, 1990.

Whitney, Craig R. "Britain Backs End to South African Sports Barriers." *The New York Times,* April 24, 1991.

Winerip, Michael. "Sign or Sit Out: School Drug Pact Angers Athletes." *The New York Times,* October 9, 1990.

Wren, Christopher S. "An Era Ends, Another Begins: South Africa to Go to Olympics." *The New York Times,* November 7, 1991.

———. "South Africa a Bit Closer to Rejoining Olympics." *The New York Times,* March 28, 1991.

Chapter 6

Associated Press. "Former Notre Dame Player Loses Suit for Reinstatement." *The New York Times,* August 18, 1990.
———. "Great Expectations." *Kennebec Journal,* November 15, 1990.
Barra, Allen. "Sack Athletic Scholarships." *The New York Times,* September 24, 1990.
Berkow, Ira. "A Focus on 'The Light of Truth.'" *The New York Times,* February 16, 1991.
———. "Syracuse May Be Added to an Untidy Laundry List." *The New York Times,* February 10, 1991.
Bissinger, J. G. "America's Youngest Professionals." *The New York Times,* November 17, 1990.
———. *Friday Night Lights.* Reading, Mass.: Addison-Wesley, 1990.
Bondy, Filip. "Basketball and Dreams in a Gym in the Bronx." *The New York Times,* April 29, 1991.
"Bright Lights, Big College Money." *The New York Times,* editorial, September 15, 1990.
George, Thomas. "Lured but Bypassed by the Draft." *The New York Times,* June 17, 1990.
Goldaper, Sam. "As Salaries in the N.B.A. Soar, Pressure to Leave College Mounts." *The New York Times,* December 29, 1990.
Kinney, Brenden. "The Scars of Playing the Game." *The New York Times,* August 26, 1990.
Rhoden, William C. "Limits Are Sought on Games, Practice." *The New York Times,* July 2, 1990.
———. "N.C.A.A. Reformers and Rumor Mill, Both at Work." *The New York Times,* January 13, 1991.
———. "N.C.A.A.'s Smoke and Mirrors." *The New York Times,* January 11, 1992.
Smith, Timothy W. "High School Tryouts for W.L.A.F.?" *The New York Times,* May 19, 1991.
Sperber, Murray. *College Sports, Inc.* New York: Henry Holt, 1990.
———. "N.C.A.A. Reforms: Barely Eligible." *The New York Times,* January 5, 1991.

Stevenson, Samantha. "Ismail to Enter N.F.L. Draft; Patriots Are Evaluating Options." *The New York Times,* January 25, 1991.

Vecsey, George. "Arthur Ashe Confronts Apocalypse." *The New York Times,* June 8, 1991.

Wallace, William N. "What a Difference a Year Can Make." *The New York Times,* May 4, 1992.

Williams, Dennis A. "Raising the Grade for Athletes." *Newsweek,* January 17, 1983.

Chapter 7

Abramowitz, Paul. "They're Not Just for Kids Anymore." *Maine Sunday Telegram,* August 12, 1990.

Anderson, Dave. "Are Your Autographs Forged?" *The New York Times,* April 30, 1991.

———. "When Mantle Had to Battle for a Raise." *The New York Times,* January 26, 1992.

Associated Press. "America Bought the Fight and Hype." *Kennebec Journal,* October 27, 1990.

———. "San Jose Seeking Stadium Support." *The New York Times,* January 22, 1992.

———. "Fans Test Players' Patience." *Kennebec Journal,* May 15, 1991.

Atkin, Ross. "Far from the Majors." *The Christian Science Monitor,* August 20, 1990.

"A Whole New Ball Game." Research by Richard Sandomir, James Rodewald, and STATS, Inc. *Sports Illustrated,* April 16, 1990.

Belinkie, Paul. "Rotisserie Baseball: Hot-Stove League Boils Over." *The New York Times,* March 25, 1991.

Black, George. "Soccer's Disease: Commercialism." *The New York Times,* July 14, 1990.

Chass, Murray. "Baseball's Giants Reach Agreement to Move to Florida." *The New York Times,* August 8, 1992.

———, "Series Is Over, but the Relish Remains." *The New York Times,* October 29, 1991.

Cobb, Nathan. "Rotiss: The Greatest Game for Baseball Fans Since Baseball," *Smithsonian,* June, 1990.

Dawidoff, Nicholas. "You (Bleep)!" *Sports Illustrated*, June 3, 1991.

Durso, Joseph. *The All-American Dollar: The Big Business of Sports.* Boston: Houghton Mifflin, 1971.

——. "War and Economy Affect Racing." *The New York Times,* February 3, 1991.

Egan, Timothy. "City Fights to Keep Its Losing Team." *The New York Times,* January 6, 1992.

Goldman, Kevin. "CBS Gets Beaned by Its Baseball Play." *The Wall Street Journal,* October 10, 1990.

King, Peter. "Inside the NFL." *Sports Illustrated,* September 24, 1990.

Landler, Mark. "The Too-Wide World of Television Sports." *Business Week,* December 10, 1990.

Lapointe, Joe. "Where, O Where, Have the Hockey Fans Gone?" *The New York Times,* December 4, 1991.

Miller, Bryan. "Food at the Ball Park: Now It's Cuisine." *The New York Times,* August 10, 1990.

Neff, Craig. "Playing the Market." *Sports Illustrated,* August 24, 1990.

Reif, Rita. "The Boys of Summer Play Ball Forever, for Collectors." *The New York Times,* February 17, 1991.

Rhoden, William C. "Tossing and Turning on the Fields of Dreams." *The New York Times,* June 30, 1991.

Rothman, Andrea. "Sports Memorabilia: A Way to Field Some Dreams." *Business Week,* August 13, 1990.

Sandomir, Richard. "And That 10-Yard Loss Was Brought to You By . . ." *The New York Times,* November 11, 1991.

——. "Vincent Sounds an Alarm on TV Revenue." *The New York Times,* November 22, 1991.

——. "What If They Held a League and No One Watched? Here's the Answer." *The New York Times,* September 18, 1992.

Sexton, Joe. "Garden Hears Advice on Tickets." *The New York Times,* October 31, 1990.

——. "Madison Sq. Garden Planning $70 Seats As Its Debts Mount." *The New York Times,* October 20, 1990.

Smith, Claire. "Sticks and Stones and Words That Do Hurt." *The New York Times,* May 15, 1991.

Smothers, Ronald. "No Hits, No Runs, One Error: The Dome." *The New York Times,* June 15, 1991.

Soloway, Steve. "Tight Budgets Put Brakes on Drivers." *Kennebec Journal,* August 5, 1990.

Steinbreder, John. "ESPN's Baseball Ratings Blues." *Sports Illustrated,* August 20, 1990.

"Support for Pro Football Contract Costs Mayor of Oakland His Job." *The New York Times,* June 7, 1990.

Swift, E. M. "Back Off!" *Sports Illustrated,* August 13, 1990.

Thomas, Robert McG., Jr. "Giants Do Some Serious Flirting with San Jose." *The New York Times,* January 16, 1992.

——. "Modified League." *The New York Times,* August 13, 1990.

——. "Red Hot on Scalping." *The New York Times,* August 5, 1990.

Vecsey, George. "Legislator Proposes a Fine Idea." *The New York Times,* April 5, 1991.

Wilstein, Steve. "American Sports a Big Business." *Kennebec Journal,* August 26, 1991.

Zoglin, Richard. "How Much Is Too Much?" *Time,* August 10, 1992.

Chapter 8

Associated Press. "Vincent Financial Plea." *The New York Times,* February 23, 1991.

Chass, Murray. "Vincent, Bowing to Owners' Will, Resigns as Baseball Commissioner." *The New York Times,* September 8, 1992.

Diaz, Jaime. "Gavaldon Retires from Pro Tennis." *The New York Times,* March 25, 1991.

Fabrikant, Geraldine. "CBS Offers to Buy 44% of Its Stock." *The New York Times,* December 13, 1990.

Finn, Robin. "Fame, Set, Match: Is It Too Much for Sampras?" *The New York Times,* August 26, 1991.

George, Thomas. "Tagliabue Looks at Dollars, Deals and N.F.L. Draft." *The New York Times,* April 18, 1991.

——. "World League and Expansion Are Put on Pause." *The New York Times,* September 18, 1992.

Guttmann, Allen. *A Whole New Ball Game*. Chapel Hill and London: University of North Carolina, 1988.

Harwitt, Sandra. "Capriati Succumbs to Pressure as Sabatini Steps to Scmifinal." *The New York Times,* January 22, 1992.

Rhoden, William C. "Coming In out of the Cold." *The New York Times,* September 24, 1991.

Sandomir, Richard. "I.R.S. Ruling Stirs Worry About Bowl Payments." *The New York Times*, December 6, 1991.

———. "Pay-Per-View Draws Top Bouts, Not Ratings." *The New York Times,* February 4, 1992.

Simpson, Janice C. "Real-Life Davids vs. Goliaths." *Time,* October 21, 1991.

Wilstein, Steve. "American Sport a Big Business." *Kennebec Journal,* August 26, 1991.

———. "Spectator Sports Face Challenges." *Kennebec Journal,* August 30, 1991.

Index

Oakland Athletics, 3, 37
Oakland Raiders, 55, 157
Okamoto, Ayako, 34, 72
Oklahoma State, 122
Olympic Games, 13–14, 21, 33, 88,
  116; discrimination policy, *v–vi*,
  112; televised, 47, 139–40, 150,
  161; women and, 13, 102, 103. *See
  also* International Olympic Committee; U.S. Olympic Committee
Owens, Jesse, 108

Pacific Southwest Championships, 105
Paige, Satchel, 108
Parker, Dave, 145
Parrish, Bernie, 54
Person, Anne, 83
Philadelphia Eagles, 77, 146, 157
Philadelphia Flyers, 146
Philadelphia Phillies, 86, 92, 157
Piniella, Lou, 99
Pittsburgh Penguins, 149
Pittsburgh Pirates, 57
Pittsburgh Steelers, 57
Players League, 36
Players' Association, 30, 93, 94
Portland Trail Blazers, 8, 148
Powell, Mike, *v*, 21
Product endorsements, 7, 55, 60, 64–
  68, 82–85, 154
Professional Bowling Association, 34
Professional Golfers Association (PGA),
  6, 34, 42, 47, 53, 109, 113, 118, 160

Quinn, Pat, 59

Radio broadcasting, 43
Ramsey, Eric, 124
Record breaking, *v*, 14, 21–22
Reserve system, 28–29, 33, 36, 59, 60,
  62, 72
Reston, James, 56
Rhoden, William, 111, 132
Rijo, José, 75
Robinson, Jackie, 109
Rose, Pete, 98, 99, 101
Rotisserie ball, 141–43

Rozelle, Alvin "Pete," 60, 63, 94
Rugby, 24, 115, 155
Running, 13, 14, 20, 53, 103
Runyan, Paul, 42
Ruth, Babe, 39, 41, 70, 71, 108, 153
Ryan, Nolan, 140

Sabatini, Gabriela, 105
St. Louis Blues, 5, 58, 59, 73
St. Louis Cardinals, 62
Salaries, 63, 70, 76, 80–81, 127, 153,
  159–60. *See also specific sports*
Sampras, Pete, 59, 64, 78, 162
San Diego Sockers, 80
San Francisco Giants, 3, 37, 50, 156,
  157
San Jose Sharks, 149
Schiller, Harvey, 71
Scholarships, 122–24, 126, 128, 129,
  136, 161
Seattle Mariners, 156, 158
Seles, Monica, 6, 7, 72
Shanahan, Brendan, 73
Shaw, Brian, 63, 75
Shoemaker, Willie, 6, 7–8, 86
Sinden, Harry, 59
Smith, Bruce, 152
Smith, Charles, 86–87
Smith, Claire, 2, 91, 111
Smoltz, John, 1–2
Smulyan, Jeff, 156
Soccer, 24, 53, 80, 155
Southern University, 113
Spalding, Albert, 26, 27, 29, 30–32,
  40, 57, 60, 70, 72, 116
Sperber, Murray, 92, 104–6, 111, 114,
  120, 122–24, 126, 127, 128, 132–33
Spira, Howard, 75, 97
Stabler, Ken, 55, 56
Stanford University, 122
Stanley Cup, 63, 149
Steinberg, Leigh, 82, 151, 163–64
Steinbrenner, George, 75, 85, 97–99
Steroids, 88–90, 93–94
Stevens, Scott, 5–6, 58, 59, 73
Stewart, Dave, 3, 58
Strange, Curtis, 6

Strawberry, Darryl, 4, 58, 69–70, 76, 141
Sullivan, Louis W., 68, 83, 84
Super Bowl, *v,* 139, 148, 152, 161, 163
Syracuse University, 130–131

Tagliabue, Paul, 46, 106, 112–13, 150–51, 159–60
Tarpley, Roy, 87
Tax, income, 48–49, 50, 123, 133, 160
Taylor, Lawrence, 4–5, 63
Teagle, Terry, 69
Television, 54–57, 106, 155; blackout rules, 45–46; cable, 140, 150–51, 161; revenues, 46–47, 50, 57
Tennis, 17, 20, 34, 64, 109, 152, 164; amateur, 115–16, 118–19; competitions, 53, 64, 83, 105; injuries, 54, 78; salaries, 6, 59, 64; sponsorship, 67–68, 69, 83; women's, 103. *See also* U.S. Tennis Association
Texas Rangers, 49, 77
Thorpe, Jim, 108, 119–20
Tour de France, 6
Track and field, 24, 53, 109, 118, 119
Tulane University, 99, 125, 127–28
Turner, Ted, 49, 81
Tyson, Mike, *v,* 82, 105, 162

Ueberroth, Peter, 76
Underwood, John, 153
University of Arkansas, 104
University of Kansas, 122
University of Michigan, 128
University of Nevada at Las Vegas (UNLV), 124, 125, 131
University of Pennsylvania, 44, 45
U.S. Boxing Association, 34
U.S. Football League, 52
U.S. Lawn Tennis Association, 34, 61
U.S. Olympic Committee, 33, 48, 71, 101–2. *See also* Olympic Games
U.S. Open (golf), 53
U.S. Open (tennis), 34, 47, 53
U.S. Professional Lawn Tennis Association, 118
U.S. Tennis Association, 8, 34, 47, 53
Utley, Mike, 77, 78

Valenzuela, Patrick, 87, 95
Valvano, Jim, 99
Vancouver Canucks, 6, 59
Vecsey, George, 85
Vincent, Fay, *vi,* 57, 75, 95, 97, 111, 151, 159, 160
Virginia Slims Tournament, 67–68, 83, 105
Vukovich family, 79

Wagner, Honus, 71, 108, 140
Walden, Jim, 126
Washington Redskins, 50, 110, 113
White, Bill, 111
Wieslander, Hugo, 120
Williams, Doug, 110
Williams, Gary, 87
Williams, John "Hot Rod," 59, 99, 125, 126, 127
Wimbledon championship, 53, 118
Wimsatt, Jim, 102
Winfield, Dave, 75, 97, 99
Women, 13, 17–18, 102–7
Women's International Pro Tennis Council, 83–84
World Basketball League (WBL), 52
World Cup, 53
World Football League, 52
World Grand Prix, 6
World Hockey Association, 52, 54
World League of American Football, 52, 129, 151
World Series, 1, 37, 43, 56–57, 151, 162
Wrestling, 13, 14, 15, 115
Wright, Harry, 26, 30
Wyche, Sam, 106–7

Ziegler, John, 95